SINGING IN THE

SINGING IN THE FIRE

Christians in Adversity

Faith Cook

THE BANNER OF TRUTH TRUST

THE BANNER OF TRUTH TRUST
3 Murrayfield Road, Edinburgh EH12 6EL
P.O. Box 621, Carlisle, Pennsylvania 17013, USA

*

© Faith Cook 1995
First Published 1995
ISBN 0 85151 684 X

*

Typeset in 10½/12pt Plantin
Printed and bound in Great Britain
by BPC Paperbacks Ltd
A member of
The British Printing Company Ltd

Contents

Acknowledgements

I am indebted to the Evangelical Library in London for supplying me with many of the books I needed for background reading for this work, and for all the help of the staff in tracking down other source materials less readily available. I would also like to express my sincere thanks to the Rev. Richard Brooks of York who has constantly urged me on by his enthusiasm for the project and has most kindly read each chapter as it was written. And again, I am especially grateful to my husband Paul, who is at once my most exacting critic and warmest encourager.

Illustrations

Foreword

We live in a day of small things. These are, by and large, superficial days rather than deep days; weak days rather than robust days; sometimes even despairing days rather than hopeful days – days when faith often burns low, courage fails, eyes grow dim and hands hang down: all of which makes the publication of Faith Cook's new book a timely event.

The question is asked and answered in the New Testament, 'Who is he that overcomes the world, but he that believes that Jesus is the Son of God?' (*1 John* 5:5). The preceding verse has announced, 'For whatever is born of God overcomes the world; and this is the victory that overcomes the world – even our faith.' And the Lord Jesus Christ himself adds an exquisite promise: 'To him who overcomes I will grant to sit with me on my throne, even as I also overcame and sat down with my Father on His throne' (*Rev.* 3:21).

Overcoming faith is the subject of this book and links the chapters together. It is the golden thread that runs through all these records of Christians facing adversity. From a wide range of different countries, generations and ages of life, the following accounts have been selected. This in itself puts us in mind of the character of God's elect, 'of all nations and kindreds and people and tongues' (*Rev.* 7:9).

Some 'Christian biographies' fail to satisfy because they fall short at the most vital point: they tell you all they can about their subject, but you learn nothing of God and the triumphs of his grace. This book, on the other hand, enables us to read of the glorious and gracious works and ways of the living God among men and women, young and old, and his dealings with poor sinners, consoling and sustaining them in all their trials. It causes us, after reading, to turn aside to worship and adore him and to cry out to him in all our need.

Many of us already have immense cause for gratitude to God for Mrs Cook's two earlier books, *Grace in Winter* and *Samuel Rutherford and his Friends*. Here, with *Singing in the Fire*, is a further reason to be thankful. As you read and reread it you will come to have your favourite passages, as I have. But oh! how the whole book thrills the soul! I am absolutely delighted to commend it, and hope that it will be read and enjoyed by multitudes, including many young people.

RICHARD BROOKS
York, April 1995

JOHN BRADFORD
Not Accepting Deliverance

Be of good comfort, brother; for we shall have a merry supper with the Lord this night!

JOHN BRADFORD

> O England! England! favoured once and blest,
> The land I love, the land that gave me birth,
> Repent, repent, O turn from error's way,
> And from those false beguiling anti-christs
> That cheat the soul; for narrow is the gate
> And hard the path that leads to endless life.
>
> And you, my brother, partner of my pain,
> With youth unburdened by the changeful years,
> Be of good comfort: though the searing heat
> Our flesh destroy, yet ere this day is done,
> By death unchained, we shall together share
> A merry supper with the Lord this night!

F.C.

I

It was 3.30 in the morning on 1 July 1555. As the eastern sky began to lighten across London it revealed a strange sight: a vast concourse of men and women astir at that early hour and each with a single purpose. Rumour had spread from mouth to mouth that John Bradford was to be burnt at the stake at four o'clock, and all were pressing towards Smithfield to witness the event. One woman, recalling that morning many years later, told how she lost both shoes in the crush and was forced to walk barefoot as far as Ludgate Hill.

Perhaps the authorities had hoped to carry out the execution of John Bradford before the people were aware of their evil deed, for Bradford was held in high affection and they feared a tumult. In the event it was not until nine o'clock in the morning that he was led out from Newgate to Smithfield to suffer.

John Bradford was born near Manchester about the year 1510. Little has been recorded of his early years but we learn from John Foxe's *Book of Martyrs* that Bradford received a good education, probably at Manchester Grammar School. Following this he entered the service of Sir John Harrington, who was Henry VIII's army treasurer, becoming highly trusted and competent in handling army finances.

1547 was to be a critical year for Bradford. Leaving Sir John's service, he became a student of law at the Inner Temple. More importantly, however, this was the year when he experienced that profound spiritual change which was to affect every part of his subsequent life. This was brought about in God's purposes through the influence of a friend and fellow student, Thomas Sampson. Like many converted in mature years, John Bradford set out for heaven with earnest zeal. Sampson records that he sold his chains, rings, brooches and jewels, symbols of his unbelieving days, and distributed the proceeds among Christians in need. Then in 1548 he left his studies at the Bar and devoted himself to theology, first at Catharine Hall, Cambridge, for a few months, and then as a Fellow at Pembroke Hall.

Only seven years of life remained for John Bradford. But such was the quality of his walk with God that his name has become a by-word for holy living: often he is referred to as 'holy Bradford'. We are told that he would not consider that he had truly prayed until he had 'felt inwardly some smiting of heart for sin and some healing of that wound by faith.' He was ever a penitent in heart and those who observed him reported that he so wept for his sins in secret that they feared he might never smile again, yet he lived so cheerfully in the public eye that it was as if he had never wept.

In 1550 John Bradford was ordained by Bishop Nicholas Ridley and became one of young Edward VI's 'roving chaplains', with particular responsibility for Manchester and the surrounding area. There followed three years of incessant and fearless preaching in the north-west of the country. 'Sharply he opened and reproved sin', records John Foxe, but his ministry had an attractive balance, for we also read, 'and sweetly he preached Christ crucified'.

Constant travel did not deter Bradford from his prolific writings. At his death five years later he left behind one hundred and twenty-one manuscripts. These included many heart-warming articles, meditations, prayers, and addresses. His complete writings, first published in 1853 by the Parker Society, were reprinted in 1978 by the Banner of Truth Trust.

John Bradford was a tall, slightly-built man with an auburn beard. One outstanding feature depicted in an early print of the Reformer published in 1620 is his earnest, if not sad, eyes. His face reflects the inner beauty of a man who lived in close communion with God. Bradford allowed himself little sleep, just one meagre meal each day, and he counted it a wasted hour if he had not been able to do good to some by pen, by word or by prayer. Into his five years of service for his God, he packed a lifetime of spiritual activity.

In 1553 the sixteen-year-old Edward VI died. To outward appearances it was a grievous set-back for the church of Jesus Christ in Britain. Since the death of Henry VIII six years earlier the gospel had made rapid progress, but with the accession of Mary, daughter of Catherine of Aragon, to the throne, the iron grip of persecution once more tightened to crush the advance of true religion in the land.

Before a month had elapsed John Bradford was arrested on some trivial charge and confined to the Tower of London, never more to walk a free man. He considered it a privilege so to suffer. Writing to console his mother after he had been there about six weeks, he says, 'I thank him more of this prison than of any parlour, yea, of any pleasure that ever I had, for in it I find God, my most sweet good God, always.' During Bradford's prison days his pen was seldom idle. In a treatise entitled *The Hurt of Hearing Mass* he set out at considerable length some of the issues for which he and other Reformers were prepared to die: issues that are now so often blurred or glossed over. Over sixty letters have been preserved which were written at this time. Throughout them Bradford expresses a willingness to suffer for the truth, coupled with a tender concern for the griefs of those who loved him. 'Ah! dear hearts, be not faint-hearted,' he wrote to close friends, 'continue to walk in the fear of the Lord, as you have well begun. At the length we shall meet together in Christ's kingdom, and there never part asunder . . . O joyful place; O place of all places desired!'

During one brief bright interval in Bradford's two-year imprisonment he was cast, inadvertently it seems, into a single cell with three fellow Reformers and future martyrs: Thomas Cranmer, Nicholas Ridley and Hugh Latimer. It is not hard to imagine with what earnestness and joy they studied the Scriptures together and encouraged one another to endure to the last. Commenting on these circumstances, Latimer was to write, 'We four were thrust into one chamber, as men not to be accounted of, but, God be thanked, to our great joy and comfort, there did we together read over the New Testament with great deliberation and painful study.'

The final ten months of Bradford's life were spent in the King's Bench Prison. From here he was brought out to face a prejudiced trial before the Lord Chancellor, Stephen Gardiner, and Bishop Tonstall. Try as they might, nothing could persuade Bradford to acknowledge the validity of the Mass. Finally on 31 January 1555, he was condemned to die.

Five months of suspense followed when Bradford expected at any moment to be brought out for execution. Every expedient was employed to break his resolve, but all to no avail. He continued to employ his time in writing: meditations, prayers, and letters of consolation. In one prayer discovered later he implored the help of God for 'one standing at the stake ready to be burnt for Christ's gospel sake.' It was a prayer abundantly answered. 'I humbly pray thee that thou wouldest aid, help, and assist me with thy strength and heavenly grace . . . that I may by my death glorify thy holy name . . .' At last on 30 June the prison keeper's wife came hurrying breathlessly into Bradford's cell exclaiming in alarm: 'O Master Bradford, I come to bring you heavy news. To-morrow you must be burnt and your chain is now a-buying.' Bradford's reply was typical of his spirit: 'I thank God for it . . . The Lord make me worthy thereof.' Late that night he was moved to a cell in Newgate.

And so he was led out through the thronging crowds to a stake long anticipated. But he did not die alone. A young man, only nineteen years of age, was appointed to be chained to the same stake. It was John Leaf from Kirby Moorside in Yorkshire. Illiterate in terms of human learning, John Leaf had been taught well by the Spirit of God and no pressure of cross-examination could bring him to deny the truths he held dear. Presented with two sheets of paper, one a recantation and the other a statement of his own words at his trial, John Leaf listened carefully as both were read to him. Then taking a pin he pricked his finger and allowed a drop of blood to fall on his own avowed confession. Such was the young man who died with John Bradford.

Approaching the stake, both men fell on their faces in one brief moment of silent prayer. 'Arise and make an end', said the sheriff impatiently, 'for the press of the people is great.' And so the martyrs were chained to the stake. Just moments before the fires were lit, John Bradford lifted up his face and hands in one last plea to his countrymen: 'O England, England, repent thee of thy sins. Beware of false anti-christs; take heed they do not deceive you.' He asked forgiveness of any he might have wronged and freely forgave those who so grievously offended against him. After begging the prayers of the people, he turned to address young John Leaf, his fellow-sufferer. The words are unforgettable: 'Be of good comfort, brother; for we shall have a merry supper with the Lord this night!'

John Foxe describes the end in these words: 'He spake no more words that any man did hear, but embracing the reeds said thus, "Strait is the way and narrow is the gate that leadeth to eternal salvation and few there be that find it."' From an early account of the martyrdom we learn that he endured the flame 'as a fresh gale of wind in a hot summer's day, confirming by his death the truth of that doctrine he had so diligently and powerfully preached during his life.' So John Leaf and John Bradford joined that 'merry supper with the Lord', and in their dying inscribed the Reformation truths more deeply on the conscience of the nation. 'Us they may prison, they may bind, and burn, as they do,' Bradford had once said, 'but our cause, religion and doctrine, which we confess, they shall never be able to vanquish and put away.'

RICHARD & ALLAN
CAMERON
Invincible Faith

It is the Lord: good is the will of the Lord, who cannot wrong me or mine, but has made goodness and mercy to follow us all our days.

ALLAN CAMERON

2

Aloud knock on the door startled old Allan Cameron and his wife, Margaret. He had little doubt that it signalled trouble for this was the year 1678 in Scotland, and all who loved the name and cause of Jesus Christ, refusing to submit to the arbitrary demands of the corrupt regime of Charles II, faced severe consequences: imprisonment, heavy fines, torture and even death.

Allan Cameron was right. There at the door stood the local sheriff's officer, sent to arrest the old man. And what was his offence? He had dared to open his humble home to believing men and women who slipped in, often under cover of darkness, and there together worshipped God in accordance with the principles of Scripture and their consciences. But such private gatherings for worship were forbidden under the Conventicles Act of 1663. Perhaps some prying neighbour had noticed the activity around the Camerons' home and had reported it. So now Allan Cameron was hustled off to stand trial for this breach of the law and Margaret was left alone.

Nestling audaciously under the shadow of Falkland Palace in Fifeshire, Allan Cameron's little cottage symbolised in its situation the great divide in seventeenth-century Scottish society. The National Covenant of 1638, sworn by the people and signed, often in blood, was the people's charter for purity of doctrine and freedom of conscience in worship. It was the reference point for much of the heroism and endurance of the Covenanters during that period of intense persecution that overtook the whole country, both north and south of the border, after the Restoration of Charles II in 1660. Falkland Palace, on the other hand, represented the ruthless arm of persecution. A favourite home of the Stuarts, it had been the place where Andrew Melville, successor to John Knox, had boldly rebuked James VI for arrogating to himself powers that belonged only to Christ – true head of the church.

But now the times were hard: and as Allan Cameron awaited trial he might well have reflected on the sorrows he and Margaret had endured. Described as a general merchant, he had lived all his life in the picturesque little Fifeshire town of Falkland. Here he had held position as a burgess, and here he and his wife had brought up their family of four. Little is known of him during this period apart from the occasional reference to him in the chronicles of the times and this brief account of his imprisonment for 'holding conventicles'. It was, however, the career of his eldest son Richard, flashing across the firmament of history like a shooting star, that lends significance to the record of the imprisonment of this merchant from Falkland on 25 August 1678.

Thinking of his family and of his own uncertain future, Cameron's mind would almost certainly have strayed to his only daughter, Marion, who, according to tradition, had been murdered by the king's dragoons for no greater offence than his own. Richard, too, was in danger. His quiet days as a schoolmaster in Falkland ended abruptly after he had listened to a field-preacher – one of those intrepid men willing to risk all to minister to the spiritual needs of the people. Powerfully converted, young Cameron joined himself to another field-preacher, John Welsh of Irongray, great-grandson of John Knox. With heart flaming with zeal for the honour of Jesus Christ,

Richard himself soon began to preach – fearlessly, even recklessly. And old Allan Cameron knew only too well the perils of such a course. Michael too, his second son, recently married, shared Richard's ardour, and, consequently, his danger. Only Alexander, then aged twenty and employed as a weaver, appeared tolerably safe.

Long months of imprisonment lay ahead of Allan Cameron. He was offered the opportunity to buy his freedom with a heavy fine, but feeling acutely the injustice of his arrest, he refused and not long afterwards was transferred to the Edinburgh Tolbooth where he remained in miserable conditions, held amongst the rabble of common offenders with little hope of either justice or mercy.

In May 1679 an event occurred which had serious repercussions on all the persecuted and fugitive Covenanters: the murder of Archbishop Sharp on Magus Moor, not far from Falkland. This act of desperate revenge executed on one known as the 'Judas of the Scottish Church' and architect of much of its anguish, was still an inexcusable evil carried out for the most part by extremists. Vengeance against the archbishop's killers unleashed a furious spate of persecution on all who called themselves Covenanters. Richard Cameron may well have decided it was a judicious moment both to leave the country and also to seek formal ordination at the hands of Robert M'Ward and his fellow ministers of the Scots Church in Rotterdam – exiles of the same persecution.

Rumours of Richard's uncompromising attitudes had reached Rotterdam before him. Some called him a fanatic, accusing him of being 'incapable of preaching anything but denunciations.' M'Ward greeted him cautiously, wishing to reserve judgment until he had heard him preach. But he soon found the rumours to be based on prejudice, and instead discovered 'a man of savoury gospel spirit, the bias of his heart lying towards a proposing of Christ and persuading to a closing with him.' After some months M'Ward and his associate ministers in Rotterdam were prepared to ordain Richard. And a strange ordination service it was! These were suffering times and no preacher could be faithful to biblical truth without inviting reprisals. Three men took part in the ordination, laying their hands on the young man; when the other two removed their hands only M'Ward's remained resting on Richard's fair head. Suddenly he declared, to the surprise of all: 'Behold, all ye beholders, here is the head of a faithful minister and servant of Jesus Christ, who shall lose the same for his Master's interest, and it shall be set up before sun and moon in the public view of the world.' These remarkable words were recorded by Patrick Walker, himself a Covenanter, in his account of the lives of three of his fellow Covenanters, a work which he published in 1727.

Cameron returned to Scotland in the autumn of 1679 with M'Ward's words ringing in his ears. He knew well that his time would probably be short, but he was calmly willing to die for the truths he held dear. The 'hill-men', as the Covenanters were sometimes called, were dispirited and divided. They had taken up arms at Bothwell Bridge and paid dearly for it in ignominious defeat and cruel retribution. 'Richie' soon became the beloved leader of the scattered remnant, which slowly regained its morale, and the more so when Donald Cargill, respected and mature, also joined them.

A born preacher, Cameron held the people spellbound with his moving sermons. Men, women and little children would steal out of their hamlets and farms to many a hidden glen to hear his passionate and consoling words as he held forth Christ to all who would take him. Young and fearless, he would stand on some rocky prominence before the expectant congregation, while guards, stationed at a distance, watched with vigilance for any approach by the king's dragoons. To the troubled he preached on such texts as, 'Come unto me all ye that labour and are heavy laden', and to the undecided, 'Ye will not come unto me that ye might have life.' We can almost hear the preacher's voice still as he pleads with the people:

Will ye take him, yea or nay? Will ye take him home with you? . . . Take the glorious Person who has occasioned our coming together here this day into this wild place. What! shall I say that any of you were not content to take him? I would fain think that some of you would take him. And if, from the bottom of your heart, ye have a mind to take him, ye shall get the earnest of the Spirit, he will in no wise cast you out. Poor vile drunkard, take him. Swearer, adulterer, liar, be what you will, we give you the call and warning to come and take him . . . What say ye? Shall I go away and tell my Master that ye will not come unto him? . . . Angels are wondering at the offer. They stand beholding with admiration that our Lord is giving you such an offer this day. They are all witnesses now, and when you are dying they shall come before your face.

At this point, we are told, the preacher wept and all the people wept with him. Reports of that sermon, and others like it, were passed from father to son and still survived over two hundred years later among the people of those districts where Cameron preached, his biographer, John Herkless, informs us.

But there was a high price on Richard Cameron's life. His offence was a double one in the eyes of the state. Not only did he preach in the open fields in defiance of the law, but he had the audacity to declare that Charles II had forfeited his privilege of kingship by his flagrant abuse of both the civil and religious rights of his people. Following a daring line of thought propounded by John Knox,

Samuel Rutherford and others, he declared that such a king was no king and, therefore, the people were not obliged to submit to his arbitrary dictates. Such talk was declared treasonable and five thousand merks in Scottish currency was offered to any who could hand over Cameron, alive or dead, with an additional three thousand merks for his brother, Michael. Little wonder that old Allan Cameron in his Edinburgh prison trembled for the lives of his sons.

'Lord, spare the green and take the ripe', was Richard Cameron's repeated prayer as he and a few faithful followers faced a menacing band of the king's dragoons at Ayrsmoss. It was his last battle. Throughout the early months of 1680 the noose had been drawing ever tighter around the outspoken preacher, and the more so after he and his small band of men had posted an open repudiation of the kingship of Charles II on the Market Cross at Sanquhar on 22 June. This act, treasonable though it might then appear, was but the precursor to the judgment of a whole nation, when James Stuart was finally driven from the throne in the Revolution of 1688.

Cameron sensed that the end was near. He must have known the dragoons were searching for him in the area and the price tag on his life was a tempting one. He and his men spent the night of 19 July in a farm at Meadowhead, in Ayrshire. When the farmer's daughter brought him water in the morning he washed his hands with extra care, remarking, 'This is their last washing, I have need to make them clean for there are many to see them.' When the girl began to cry he chided her with these words: 'Weep not for me, but for yourself and yours and for the sins of a sinful land, for you have many melancholy, sorrowful and weary days before you.'

From the farm Cameron rode some miles eastwards along the valley of the River Ayr, until he reached the wild and lonely moors known as Ayrsmoss. Here the king's dragoons came upon him. He and his men were heavily outnumbered and inadequately matched against the superior force of arms. 'Come, Michael, let us fight it out to the last', called Richard to his brother. And to the little party of some twenty men on foot and about forty on horseback, he cried out, 'Be encouraged all of you to fight it out valiantly; to all of you who fall this day I see heaven's gates cast wide open to receive them.' It was a brave, but hopeless, fight and the little band was soon routed. Nine lay dead, six were taken prisoner and the rest escaped, some badly wounded, across the wild grassland surrounding Ayrsmoss. Cameron's head and hands were severed from his body and thrown into a sack, to be carried to Edinburgh, there to be crudely displayed on the Netherbow gate – an intended object lesson in the fate of those who dared defy the religious system of the day. His body, with that of Michael and the others who lay dead, was thrown into a shallow grave.

One more act of cruelty remained: an act designed to lacerate the heart of an old man. Before fixing Cameron's head and hands high up on the Netherbow gate, the soldiers called at the Tolbooth to show the hands to Richard's father, Allan Cameron. 'Whose hands are these?' the soldier enquired callously, holding them in front of his eyes. Richard had been a fair-skinned man and his father recognised the mutilated hands instantly. Taking them in his own, he kissed them and wept. 'I know them, I know them', he replied at last. 'They are my son's, my dear son's. It is the Lord: good is the will of the Lord, who cannot wrong me or mine, but has made goodness and mercy to follow us all our days.' Such words of invincible faith deserve a permanent place in the annals of the courage and endurance of the people of God.

The days were dark indeed. Words of one stern old Covenanter, spoken when he heard of the slaughter at Ayrsmoss, expressed the unspoken desires of many: 'Oh to be wi' you, Richie!'

WANG MING-DAO
Baffled to Fight Better

There are so many stones in the brook that you cannot count them. Yet in every ten you cannot find more than one or two that are useable. There was no room in David's pouch for stones which had not been polished smooth. The process of attrition was essential. In the same way those believers who have not yet experienced trials and afflictions, and who have not yet been disciplined by God, are still not ready for his use. What I am anxious to know is whether I myself am qualified to be a 'smooth stone' in the hand of my God.

WANG MING-DAO

3

A young man climbed a rickety ladder and peered anxiously over the compound wall. The sight that greeted him confirmed his worst fears. Firmly stationed on the other side of the wall stood numerous armed soldiers awaiting the order to attack.

It was June 1900, the year of the Boxer Risings in China. Inflamed by fear and hatred of foreign influence and power, and egged on by the Empress Dowager, Tzu-Hsi, the Boxers had rampaged though the land killing as many missionaries and Chinese Christians as they could find. Nearly two thousand Protestant Christians and many more Roman Catholics had perished. In addition, almost two hundred missionaries were hunted out and killed before allied forces halted the massacre. Wang Dzu-Hou was a young doctor who worked at the missionary hospital in Peking (now Beijing). His life, with that of his wife and little daughter, was in imminent danger and so, with many other missionaries and local Christians, he had taken refuge within the Legation Quarter. And now the Boxers were right outside the walls.

Trembling with fear, Wang Dzu-Hou returned to his wife and child to report what he had seen. Timid by disposition, he anticipated a cruel and merciless death and his fears soon gained control. Regardless of the fate of his wife, who was shortly expecting another child, that night Dzu-Hou hanged himself.

A month later, Dzu-Hou's wife, still sheltering in the Legation Quarters, gave birth to a son. After the Boxer

Risings were finally quelled later that year, the refugees were able to return to their homes, but for Dzu-Hou's widow there was no home to which she could return, for with her husband's death accommodation at the hospital was no longer available.

It was an inauspicious beginning to life for little Wang Ming-Zi (a name he later changed); and the more so because his mother proved inept at some of her household duties: her children were often ill through lack of adequate nourishment. But God had purposes of grace for this child and his long life was to span the greater part of the twentieth century, guiding and directing the Chinese church through critical days of its development and suffering.

Wang Ming-Zi was a serious child. Suffering frequent illness, he longed to know of a life free from the scourge of death. Timorous by nature like his father before him, the fear of death often haunted his young mind. In his own words, his early years were passed 'chaotically, unintelligibly, confusedly, without faith, without purpose, without hope.' But a change was soon to come. In 1914 a school friend pointed the troubled boy to Christ, who could 'release those who through fear of death were all their lifetime subject to bondage.' The change was radical. 'I began to hate all sin and unrighteousness. I began to long for a life of purity and goodness', he recorded.

If Wang Ming-Zi suffered from physical fears, morally he had the courage of a lion. Even as a small child he resisted bullying: when the older boys at his school shaved the heads of all the younger boys, Ming-Zi alone retained his healthy crop of black hair as he calmly threatened to use the scissors to blind anyone who attempted to touch his hair. This natural characteristic was one which God was to use in the leadership of his persecuted people in China.

Not long after his conversion Wang Ming-Zi was exercised in his mind over the call of God to the ministry. Standards of preaching were low and there was little kudos attached to such a calling. In addition, Wang had a burning ambition to become a politician. For three years he engaged in a controversy with God over this issue until eventually, during a period of serious illness, he bowed his will to God's will. Finally in 1920 he marked his response to the call of God by changing his name to Wang Ming-Dao, meaning 'Testifier to the Way'.

By this time Wang Ming-Dao had been engaged as a teacher in a Presbyterian boarding school. His influence on staff and pupils alike was profound as he resolutely determined to please God, cost what it may. And it proved a costly path for in January 1921 Ming-Dao became convinced that he should be baptized by immersion. He had never heard of the practice before, but after a friend spoke to him about it, he studied the Scriptures and became convinced that this was the course of action he must take. The principal of the school warned Wang that if he were baptized in this way, it would cost him his job. Learning later that he was still determined, the principal promptly offered him his train fare home and dismissed him from that moment.

On a bitterly cold January day a little group of people could be seen making their way up the hillside in search of some unfrozen stream. Finding a small waterfall cascading down into a turbulent pool, four students and Wang Ming-Dao were all baptized, their garments freezing as stiff as boards as they emerged from the icy water.

Wang Ming-Dao's peremptory dismissal left him without work, so he returned to his home in Peking and lived with his mother and sister. Here he gave himself to diligent study of the Scriptures in preparation for the ministry. Occasionally there were opportunities to preach and as Ming-Dao gained experience, he responded to requests to preach in far-flung parts of the country. As he travelled further afield, his name became known in some of the remote areas of that vast land. His style was simple, forthright and deeply disturbing. Fearlessly he rebuked sin and challenged the low standards he found among professing Christian churches wherever he went. This often led to unpopularity. Bitter calumnies were heaped on the head of the young preacher while others called him proud, arrogant and self-righteous. Wang Ming-Dao himself commented, 'Derision, misunderstanding, scoffing, persecution, grief – I have tasted them again and again.'

In 1924 Wang Ming-Dao began a Bible study for a handful of believers living near his home. From week to week the numbers increased and within a few months more than seventy people were gathering together. From these small beginnings sprang Wang Ming-Dao's influential Peking ministry and in 1937 the Christians' Tabernacle was erected, seating five hundred people.

In addition to his preaching ministry Wang Ming-Dao responded to repeated requests for written notes of his messages by preparing some of his sermons for publication. When at last the necessary permission to publish was granted, the *Spiritual Food Quarterly* was born. This important periodical carried the preached message to homes and congregations right across China. In the barren years after 1949 when all religion was suppressed and its preachers silenced, the written word could still minister effectively to the hearts of God's needy people. Like his preaching, these printed messages were forthright, biblical and earnest. Though possibly lacking in profundity, none who read them could fail to be comforted, edified and challenged.

Late in 1925, during one of his preaching tours, Wang Ming-Dao first met Jing-Wun, the attractive seventeen-year-old daughter of the Christians who gave him hospitality. Regardless of the age difference Ming-Dao was drawn to her and the following year they were engaged and eventually married in 1928. The early years of their married life were fraught with problems. Ming-Dao's mother and sister, neither of whom were believers, showed unaccountable and continual hostility towards the young bride whom Ming-Dao brought to the family home. In Chinese style the family continued living under the same roof for nine years despite unabated friction. Only after the completion of the Tabernacle in 1937 did Ming-Dao and his family move into their home on the church premises. Though temperamentally far different from her husband, Jing-Wun proved a true help-meet, often strengthening Ming-Dao when his courage wavered in some crisis.

In 1937 came the Japanese occupation of China with its cruelty, deprivations and widespread suffering for the people. Only one week after the formal opening of the Christians' Tabernacle, the Japanese armies entered Peking. In spite of this, Wang Ming-Dao's work was allowed to progress largely unhindered throughout the next eight years. Peace with Japan was eventually achieved in 1945, but it heralded for China a yet more momentous conflict which was destined to cast its long shadow across the remainder of the century.

Mao Tse-Tung, Chairman of the Chinese Communist Party had been steadily consolidating his position in the country districts and winning support for his Marxist ideals since 1927. Now with the nation weakened by war with Japan and corruption rife within Chiang Kai-Shek's Nationalist regime, conditions were propitious for a final onslaught. Intermittent fighting disturbed the nation for the next four years until at last the communist flag was hoisted over Peking in January 1949 as Chiang Kai-Shek fled the country. On 1 October the city was proclaimed the new capital of the People's Republic of China by Mao Tse-Tung.

A dark day for the Chinese Christian church, it brought with it intense persecution for all Bible-believing men and women who refused to compromise their faith. From that day on Christ's warning that a man's foes would be those of his own household became literally true. Parents were ready to betray their children, and children their parents, in an attempt to curry favour with the new government.

For many years God had been preparing the Chinese church for this baptism of suffering into which it was now plunged. Faithful missionaries had toiled indefatigably, often in remote and unyielding areas, seeing few tangible results for their labour. But it was seed well sown, which was to grow silently despite persecution. More than this, God had raised up Chinese pastors – men of ability and godliness who had taught the people both by preaching and the written word: men of the calibre of John Sung, David Yeng, and, of course, Wang Ming-Dao. The *Spiritual Food Quarterly* had been in circulation for almost twenty-five years and many of these messages were recalled and reread when the people faced a famine of the Word of God. Some of the sermons seemed to carry an almost prophetic note, as if the preacher had been secretly prepared by God in the themes he chose. Preaching on Peter's denial of Christ, Wang Ming-Dao showed tenderness and sensitivity towards believers who might fail in the hour of trial: 'There are many saints like Peter. In a moment of weakness they stumble and fall; they are guilty of giving offence to their Lord . . . At such a time their greatest need is to be aware of the Lord's forgiveness and pardon; to become conscious of the Lord's compassion and love.'

The Three-Self Patriotic Movement (TSPM) was an

instrument devised by the new communist government to unite all Chinese churches under the banner of patriotism to the state. Many church leaders joined in, though often reluctantly, suspecting some hidden agenda, but not realising it to be the tool of the state to sift and destroy the Christian church. The principles of the TSPM – self-government, self-support and self-propagation – were introduced as a manifesto to which all churches were expected to subscribe. These principles in themselves were ones which Wang had long embraced, but the context in which the people were now required to subscribe to them was designed specifically to bring the church under the heavy hand of atheistic government policy. Wang Ming-Dao's reaction to this demand was characteristic of the man: he denounced it and boldly called on others to join him in this stand. But there were few left to do so. One by one the voices of faithful church leaders had been silenced and their people scattered. Wang could now say sadly: 'We have nothing! no pastors, no churches, no Bibles, . . . nothing! We only have God. Therefore we go to him in desperation.'

Tension between the TSPM, representing the government, and the respected preacher of the Christians' Tabernacle rose steadily, and early in 1954 a meeting was called, 'inviting' Wang Ming-Dao's erstwhile colleagues to accuse him. But his popularity with the people, and particularly with the students who still crowded to hear him preach, made any move against him premature. Now, however, no printer would dare accept his material, and Wang was obliged to set up the type himself for the *Spiritual Food Quarterly*, often labouring far into the night. And so to encourage frightened believers to remain steadfast, he wrote in July, 1955:

We are ready to pay any price to preserve the Word of God and we are equally willing to sacrifice anything in order to preach the Word of God . . . Dear brothers and sisters, let us be strong through the mighty power of our Lord . . . Let us be prepared to be faithful to the Lord at any cost . . . Don't be cowards! Don't be weary! Don't give way! Don't compromise! The battle is indeed furious . . . but God's glory will be manifest there.

But later that month another accusation meeting was called. Now Wang Ming-Dao knew his liberty could only be short-lived. On 7 August he preached a sermon – in fact it was his last – on 'The Son of Man is betrayed into the hands of sinners', and at the close of the service he distributed printed copies of his message. It contained these heroic words: 'We shall make whatever sacrifice is required of us in being faithful to God. Regardless of how others may twist the truth and slander us, *we because of our faith shall remain steadfast.*'

Retribution was prompt and ruthless. That very night, past midnight, Wang Ming-Dao and Jing-Wun were rudely awakened. They had little doubt of what lay ahead as they were arrested, bound and hustled off to prison. Here Wang Ming-Dao was condemned as a counter-revolutionary and sentenced to fifteen years' imprisonment. He was to be separated from Jing Wun, who was also to be held in prison. The Tabernacle was closed down a few weeks later.

Chinese Christians who survived imprisonment under the communist regime – and many did not – are reluctant to speak of their experiences. But faces prematurely aged, bodies and minds broken under torture and relentless brainwashing techniques tell their own tale. To dwell on their sufferings could endanger the fragile degree of toleration now permitted in China. Wang Ming-Dao was fifty-five years of age and at the height of his usefulness as a spiritual leader when he was imprisoned. He emerged twenty-three years later, a frail old man, deaf and nearly blind.

During the silent years Christians in the West scarcely knew whether Wang was alive or dead, but God preserved him as an extraordinary testimony to the power of the grace of God to keep a man in circumstances beyond mere human endurance. Through all those years of suffering this faithful Christian pastor was deprived of his Bible and of any contact with fellow Christians. Questioned afterwards about his ordeal, Wang too was reticent, and Jing-Wun ever vigilant, in case any indiscreet word from her husband could expose him to further suffering. But the sweet triumphant peace written on his features ascribed the honour of such a conquest of grace over nature to God alone.

It had not always been so. During the early months of his imprisonment the pressure on Wang Ming-Dao to capitulate had been intense. His captors knew well that if Wang could be induced to deny his profession of faith, it would be a serious blow to the whole of the Chinese church. Day and night, bribes, threats, insinuations were aimed with deadly accuracy to undermine this good man's resolve. In a foul cell, bombarded by ceaseless political propaganda and exposed to the taunts of his fellow prisoners, Wang Ming-Dao's steadfast spirit began to waver. But, above all, it was the venomous darts of the Wicked One, that great enemy of souls, who rejoices when the godly fall, that snapped the fragile threads of his resolve. Into his troubled mind Satan injected insidious doubts: doubts about the very existence of God. Robbed of spiritual certainty, he was now an easy target. As that tumultuous year of 1955 drew to a close, Wang wrote an appeal for clemency based on a willingness to co-operate with the authorities.

His treatment changed instantly. Now every consideration

was afforded to the unhappy man: warmth, good food and improved conditions. Still Wang refused to submit entirely and write the false statements required of him which would procure his release. Since his conversion forty years earlier, he had abhorred lying. How could he now stoop to such an expedient? But in the summer of 1956 he heard that Jing-Wun's life was in danger. Weakened by distress and under-nourishment, she could not survive without a change of circumstances, so he was told. Then Wang wrote all that was demanded of him – page after page he wrote, scarcely aware of what he was doing. He agreed to join the Three-Self Patriotic Movement and to preach on its behalf. Tormented by his betrayal of all that was dear to him and by his mendacity (for he had no ultimate intention of fulfilling these undertakings), Wang determined to take his own life as soon as he and Jing-Wun were free.

And so on 30 September 1956 they released him. But it brought no relief: Wang Ming-Dao had now become bound and burdened in spirit. He complied almost automatically with every demand, even reading in public the report he had been forced to write. The ultimate ignominy came when his confession appeared in print in the TSPM magazine, *Heavenly Wind*. Now he had betrayed his Lord and Master before the world. Wang, wounded in spirit, became distraught and ill. The emphasis of his ministry over the years had tended to be a little rigid – even legal; so now, having fallen short of his own high standards, he found it hard to lay hold on the forgiving grace of God. It is said that he wandered distractedly around the streets near his home muttering, 'I am Peter . . . I am Peter', as he thought of Peter's denial of Christ and even, 'I am Judas . . . I am Judas'.

'When will Wang Ming-Dao begin to preach for the TSPM?' the government wondered. The months passed.

Gradually it became clear that this was a step that Wang had no intention of taking. He had only been lying in order to gain his freedom; clearly, they concluded, he must be 'counter-revolutionary' still. Knowing it would not be long before he was re-arrested, Wang and his wife reported to the authorities confessing that the statement he had made was false. Without delay they were cast back into jail. This time it was life-imprisonment for Wang, and for his wife, fifteen years.

For days, perhaps weeks, he could not tell how long, Wang lay in his cell in a state of abject despair. He had sinned, he had betrayed Christ: bereft of all comfort there now seemed little purpose in living. It was at this point of deep dejection that God in mercy shone a ray of light into his gloom. A verse of Scripture, memorised long ago, filtered into his mind:

Do not rejoice over me, my enemy; when I fall, I will arise; when I sit in darkness the LORD will be a light to me. I will bear the indignation of the LORD because I have sinned against him, until he pleads my cause' (*Micah* 7:9).

Slowly Wang Ming-Dao came to the view, perhaps over-severe, that the sentence of life-imprisonment meted out to him was not from the government at all, but was sent by God as a chastisement for his weakness and betrayal. But thankfully he realised that this sentence, unlike the vindictive government penalty, carried with it a clause of hope: '. . . until he pleads my cause.' Now he would endure his punishment with a different spirit. Hope returned. Soon he was removed to the prison clinic to recover health and here, instead of the filth and darkness of the cell, sunlight penetrated his ward. His mind cleared and Wang now took up his pen to write once more – not a confession of his supposed errors, but instead a bold statement of faith. This was the true Wang Ming-

Dao and Christians, distressed by his fall, took courage again.

Year succeeded year, but never again would Wang Ming-Dao deny his Saviour. The Cultural Revolution of 1966–79, which aimed to crush the spirit of the Chinese people and to extinguish the Christian church altogether, intensified his sufferings. Sometimes he was seriously ill, often mistreated, always denied access to any means of grace, but Wang did not waver. To what did he attribute his ability to overcome? It was to the sustaining power of the Word of God, memorised in early years. In his own words, 'It was the Word of God that gave me the very best moment of my life when I overcame my lies . . . If it were not for God's protection I would be dead by now, but it was the Word of God that rescued me.'

In September 1976, came the death of Chairman Mao and only a month later the 'Gang of Four' orchestrated by Mao's ruthless wife, was swept from power. The Cultural Revolution was crumbling and with it the implicit faith of the people in Mao's policies. With the return of Deng Xiaoping's more pragmatic regime, the prison doors began to swing open and in 1979 Wang Ming-Dao, emaciated but triumphant, was freed at last. The remaining years of his life were spent quietly in Shanghai with his wife, Jing-Wun. Before he died in July 1991 at the age of ninety-one, God permitted his faithful servant to witness the astonishing revival of the church of Jesus Christ in China, and to know that the Lord had indeed pleaded his cause.

SUSANNAH SPURGEON
A Ministry of Love

When the fire of affliction draws songs of praise from us, then indeed are we purified, and our God is glorified . . . Singing in the fire! Yes! God helping us, if that is the only way to get harmony out of these hard apathetic hearts, let the furnace be heated seven times hotter than before.

SUSANNAH SPURGEON

Now I, once blessed by favoured years,
Must tread a path of pain and tears;
Yet with reluctant stubborn heart
Contend against God's ways,
Until the fires of suffering draw
A hymn of faith not heard before
From out the seven-fold blaze;
So let my God be glorified,
My sinning soul be purified –
A sacrifice of praise.

F.C.

4

The debt which Christianity owes to Charles Haddon Spurgeon is incalculable. Called the Prince of Preachers, Spurgeon's influence through his printed sermons and numerous writings can still be discovered worldwide. 1992 marked the centenary of his death and commemorative addresses were given in many parts of the United Kingdom and also in other countries. Of necessity, the influence and support of his wife Susannah, could not often be mentioned in any detail. It is not inappropriate, therefore, to include a tribute to this woman, remarkable in her own right, who made so important a contribution both to her husband's ministry and to the lives of countless other preachers and their families.

Born in January 1832, Susannah Thompson was slightly more than two years older than her well-known husband. Her parents occasionally attended New Park Street Chapel, in Southwark, London, and Susie would then accompany them, listening to the preaching of James Smith – better known for his Cheltenham ministry. Some of Susie's earliest childhood memories surrounded that pulpit in New Park Street. Unable from her pew to see the door behind the pulpit, she was at first mystified as to how the preacher unaccountably 'appeared' at the beginning of the service. Even when initiated into the secrets of 'the door', she continued to indulge her childish imagination. And it was through that same door that 'the boy preacher of the Fens' – the boy who was to be her future husband – made his first unforgettable appearance.

Even as a young child Susie had shown that spiritual sensitivity which became so marked a characteristic in mature years. As she watched the pastor, James Smith, conducting baptismal services, she confessed to 'wondering with tearful longing whether I should ever be able thus to confess my faith in the Lord Jesus.' It was, however, under the preaching of S. B. Bergne, taking for his text, 'The word is near you, even in your mouth and in your heart' (*Rom.* 10:8), that Susannah was converted and could write: 'From that service I date the dawning of true light in my soul.'

On 11 December 1853, the nineteen-year-old Charles Haddon Spurgeon was invited to preach at New Park Street Chapel for the first time. Susannah was staying with her friends, Thomas Olney and his wife at the time, but declined to attend the morning service with them: her spiritual life, as she later confessed, was at a low ebb. The astonishing reports, however, with which the Olneys returned so filled the girl with curiosity that she decided to accompany them in the evening. Susannah Thompson was clearly unimpressed, even shocked, by her first sight of the young preacher: 'The huge black satin stock, the long badly trimmed hair, and the blue pocket handkerchief with white spots . . . these attracted most of my attention and I fear awakened some feelings of amusement'. Then she admits sadly, 'I was not spiritually-minded enough to understand his earnest presentation of the gospel and his powerful pleading with sinners.'

When Spurgeon finally accepted the pastorate at New Park Street, Susannah began to attend more frequently, gradually overcoming her prejudices. Through his preaching and personal conversations, held when they met at the home of the Olneys, her spiritual life was quickened and restored. She was impressed by his evident concern for her growth in grace and especially when he presented her with an illustrated copy of *The Pilgrim's Progress*, inscribed: 'Miss Thompson, With desires for her progress in the blessed pilgrimage, from C. H. Spurgeon, April 20, 1854.'

Less than two months after this, Susannah joined a group from New Park Street, including Charles, attending an opening ceremony for the splendid Crystal Palace. While they were waiting for proceedings to begin Charles, who was sitting by Susannah, suddenly drew her attention to a poem in a book he was reading, which began:

> *Seek a good wife of thy God*
> *for she is the best gift of His providence.*

Susie could not fail to understand the significance of the words. Moments later came a low voice, whispering in her ear, 'Do you pray for him who is to be your husband?' After the ceremony the pair escaped from the rest and wandered together in the grounds of the Crystal Palace. Such is the story of the unconventional start to a romance true and deep which bound Charles and Susie together for the rest of their lives.

To be the chosen partner of one whose path was to lead to eminence, adulation, blame, but above all remarkable spiritual usefulness, was a high privilege, but also an exacting challenge. Before many weeks had passed, Susannah began her apprenticeship in these demanding spheres. Shy and retiring by temperament, she found herself thrust in a moment into the public eye with a multitude of men and women seemingly agog for a glimpse of the girl that the young preacher, now the talk of London, had picked to be his bride. It was a yet harder lesson to discover that her preferences and pleasure must always be subservient to the one great end to which Charles was dedicated – his preaching ministry.

Susannah recounts with amusement some of her early experiences, most notably the occasion when she accompanied Charles to a service near her home at which he was due to preach. They arrived together by cab but as they went up a stairway to the meeting, so great was the throng of eager worshippers that Charles was swept away from Susannah and, totally oblivious of her predicament, entered some vestry. Lost and struggling in the crowd, Susannah was at first bewildered, then hurt and finally very angry. She left the meeting and returned home, where her wise mother tried to soothe her indignant and injured feelings. When Charles returned at the close of the service anxiously enquiring for Susie, he was told of the incident. But for Susannah it was a lesson well learnt, for she comments, 'I do not recollect ever again seeking to assert my right to his time and attention when any service for God demanded them.'

On 8 January 1856, Charles and Susannah were married. Charles stood at the pinnacle of his early popularity but, aware of the pitfalls of pride, he had written to Susannah not long before the wedding: 'I tremble at the giddy height on which I stand, and could wish myself unknown, for indeed I am unworthy of all my honours and fame.' It was no easy thing to become the wife of such a man and as the wedding morning dawned Susie could be found on her knees earnestly seeking divine help for the life that lay ahead of her. By eight o'clock in the morning the crowds were gathering, and long before the service was due to begin hundreds of eager well-wishers had to be turned away.

A brief honeymoon was spent in Paris and then Charles and Susannah returned to their first home together in the New Kent Road. With characteristic consideration for her husband's work Susannah insisted that the best room in the house should be used as his study – a practice she maintained in all the homes they shared.

Before many weeks had passed, Susannah entered enthusiastically into a new and cherished plan which was filling Charles' mind. He wished to provide facilities for basic education for young men who appeared to have preaching gifts but had been deprived of early educational opportunity. Despite their slender resources, Susannah was anxious to contribute towards the cost of the venture and began to economise and save out of her own house-keeping fund. Sometimes she scarcely knew how to meet the bills as they came in, but the experience of being in difficult circumstances proved invaluable training for that work which God intended for her in later years. One student was accepted in 1856 and began his training under the direction of George Rogers at Camberwell. Soon the number increased to eight, and then grew until nearly one hundred men were enrolled. So began the *Pastor's College* – a work always dear to both Susannah and Charles.

As 1856 wore on, the crowds clamouring to hear Spurgeon preach steadily mounted. The enlarged New Park Street Chapel proved inadequate, and the congregation was obliged to return to the Exeter Hall for the evening services where it had worshipped in 1855 while further extensions were being made. But as his popularity grew so the censures and calumnies from the secular press and elsewhere multiplied proportionately. Caricatures and slander were the order of the day and Spurgeon inevitably winced at times for he was only twenty-two years of age. If it was hard for him to ignore the abuse, it was even harder for Susie. 'My heart alternately sorrowed for him and flamed with indignation against his detractors', she confessed in later years. At last

[39]

she hit upon an expedient that would help them both. At a time before wall motto texts were popular, she framed the words of Christ on rejoicing in persecution (*Matt.* 5:11–12), and hung them in Charles' study.

In September 1856 twin sons, Thomas and Charles, were born. There seemed little to mar the joy of Susannah and Charles, but within four weeks a shadow fell across their happy lives that for ever afterwards they referred to as 'the great catastrophe'. October 19 was to be the first night that Charles preached at the Surrey Gardens Music Hall, reputed to seat at least ten thousand people. Susannah, still weak after the birth of the boys, remained at home, though doubtless her thoughts followed her young husband as he stood in front of that vast concourse of people. To her surprise she heard footsteps approaching the house long before the service was due to end. It was one of the deacons and from his face Susannah knew he carried sad news. Quickly and sympathetically he told her of the malicious trick carried out in the middle of the service by unknown persons who had cried, 'Fire, fire! the galleries are falling.' This had led to panic and stampede, leaving seven dead and twenty-eight others injured, some seriously. When Charles was eventually brought home, the anguish of that evening's experience had altered his entire appearance.

For some days he was inconsolable. It was a night of weeping for the young couple and at times it seemed as if Charles' reason was so affected that he might never recover or preach again. But God intervened and as Charles paced to and fro in the garden of the home to which he had resorted, the words of Scripture in Philippians 2:9–11 flashed into his troubled mind. Stopping in his tracks, he exclaimed with the old light returning to his eyes: 'How foolish I have been! Why, what does it matter what becomes of me if the Lord shall but be glorified?' He then repeated the words of Scripture which had brought such instantaneous relief: 'If Christ be exalted, let him do as he pleases with me; my one prayer shall be that I may die to self and live wholly for him and for his honour.' 'In that moment his fetters were broken', Susannah later recorded, though she admitted that never again did Charles regain his same youthful vigour and that the calamity left its scar upon him for the rest of his life.

In 1857 Charles and Susannah moved from their home in the New Kent Road to the seclusion of Nightingale Lane, in Clapham, then a delightful rural district. Escape from the public eye had become important as Spurgeon's ministry continued to attract an eager response from the people and also unremitting harassment from the press. The years at this home, called Helensburgh House, were peaceful ones for Susannah and Charles. 'We lived in the dear old house in Nightingale Lane for many happy years', wrote Susannah. 'I think they must have been the most unshadowed by care and sorrow of all the years of our married life.'

During the early part of this period Spurgeon preached at the Surrey Gardens Music Hall, overcoming his natural reluctance to do so which sprang from his memory of the disaster. This continued until the New Park Street congregation at last had a building of its own adequate to accommodate the crowds wishing to attend. The Metropolitan Tabernacle, a vast, well-proportioned and attractive building which could seat between five and six thousand worshippers, was opened free of debt in March 1861. Here Charles was to preach for the next thirty years. Susannah played her full part in the life of the church, in particular giving valued help at baptismal services to the women and girl candidates. Whenever possible she accompanied Charles on his journeys overseas, which became increasingly necessary as a relief from the pressure of his life. Her work outside the home was never allowed to take precedence over her responsibilities to her twin sons. In later years both Thomas and Charles gladly acknowledged the formative influence of their mother's life on their development and traced their early conversion to God to her faithful instruction.

These years proved a quiet lull before an impending storm, for in 1868, when the twins were twelve and Susannah only thirty-six years of age, she suffered a serious set-back in health – a condition that left her a semi-invalid for the rest of her life. 'Henceforth', she tells us, 'for many years I was a prisoner in a sick chamber, and my beloved had to leave me when the strains of his many labours compelled him to seek rest far away from home.' A degree of self-sacrifice was now required of this young woman beyond anything she had previously known and she rose to the challenge.

Susannah received the best medical help then available, undergoing two major operations performed by Sir James Simpson of Edinburgh, famed for the discovery of chloroform. With typical Victorian reticence, Susannah gives no details as to the exact nature of her condition. Beyond doubt, however, her problems arose from complications following the birth of the twins. Childbirth still carried a high degree of risk in the mid-nineteenth century, and the delivery of twins would prove exceptionally difficult. Sir James was the leading gynaecologist of his day and a pioneer of surgical repair operations. But obstetrics, as a branch of surgery, was still in its infancy, and it is clear that despite all Sir James' skill, the operations were not entirely successful. Any surgery at that time was life-threatening and often in an experimental stage, but Susannah faced the prospect of life or death with calm resignation. Sir James made no charge for his professional services; when Spurgeon enquired about his fee, he commented, possibly jokingly, that though his normal fee would have been one thousand guineas, he would only make that charge when Spurgeon became Archbishop of Canterbury!

Susannah's recovery was only partial and she experienced frequent and prolonged periods of pain. To this time belongs the charming story of 'the opal ring and singing bullfinch'. When Charles, grieved by Susie's continual sufferings, asked her what gift he could bring her as he set off yet again for one of his many preaching engagements, Susie replied, half playfully, 'an opal ring and a singing bullfinch.' Charles shook his head sadly at such a request, but Susie tells the story of the way both these quaint wishes were met: 'a direct love-gift from a pitiful Father.'

While Susannah was convalescing in Brighton in 1869 the much-loved family home in Nightingale Lane was demolished, to be replaced by a new and better Helensburgh House, more suited to the needs of both Susannah, in her invalid condition, and the increasing demands created by Spurgeon's ministry. Charles, with amazing concern for every detail that might bring Susie a little comfort, personally presided over the choice of furnishings, incorporating many small luxuries calculated to please her. How great was her delight when she was well enough to return home to discover these evidences of his thought. Complications arising from Susannah's ailment made it difficult for her to lead an active life or to venture from her home. Most of her days had, therefore, to be spent seated in an easy chair, probably on the recommendation of the current, rather restrictive, medical opinion.

These years of suffering with many enforced separations from Charles often led to distress and tension for Susannah, and occasionally in her autobiographical writings she allows the reader a glimpse into the turmoil of her mind as she wrestled against anxiety, pain and self-pity. Lying on her bed one dark winter evening after a period of prolonged illness, Susannah found querulous and unbelieving thoughts invading her mind, destroying her spiritual peace: 'Why does God so often send sharp and bitter pain to visit me? Why does my Lord thus deal with his child?' The answer, unexpected yet plain, came in the form of a parable. Into the silence of the room, disturbed only by the noise of the crackling log burning in the hearth, broke a sound, clear and musical, not unlike birdsong. 'We listened again and heard the faint plaintive notes, so sweet, so melodious, yet mysterious enough to provoke for a moment our undisguised wonder.' Suddenly Susannah's friend exclaimed, 'It comes from the log on the fire.' She was right.

The fire was letting loose the imprisoned music from the old oak's inmost heart! . . . Ah, thought I, when the fire of affliction draws songs of praise from us, then indeed are we purified, and our God is glorified . . . Singing in the fire! Yes! God helping us, if that is the only way to get harmony out of these hard apathetic hearts, let the furnace be heated seven times hotter than before.

In 1875 Susannah was directed, almost accidentally it would seem, into that important service for the kingdom of God which became uniquely her own. When Charles showed his wife a proof copy of his first volume of *Lectures to My Students*, Susannah was delighted. 'I wish I could place it in the hands of every minister in England' was her enthusiastic response. 'Then why not do so: how much will you give?' came the unexpected reply. Susie was taken aback but began to wonder how she could help to distribute the book. Then she remembered: there was a small collection of crown pieces lying in an upstairs drawer. It would be just enough to cover the cost of one hundred copies of the work. Such was the beginning of 'Mrs Spurgeon's Book Fund'.

These were days when many faithful ministers of Jesus Christ were required to live on a pittance. With scarcely enough money to feed and clothe their families, books became a luxury that must frequently be sacrificed. With minds impoverished through lack of stimulating reading material, their ministries often suffered in consequence, and discouragement, even despair, was widespread.

When Susannah's plan to send books to needy pastors became known through the pages of the church magazine, *The Sword and the Trowel*, gifts and unneeded books for redistribution began to flow in. Soon Susannah was fully engaged in packing up and posting parcels to many grateful pastors. In order to discover those in the most acute need, Susannah asked that only men whose stipend was below £150 a year should apply for books. Letters of need from all over the country and from men of every denomination saddened Susannah as she learnt of countless pastors struggling to subsist on less than £50 a year.

Soon copies of *The Treasury of David* were added to the regular contents of the parcels and by the end of the first year, in spite of periods of serious illness, Susannah had distributed over three thousand books. Letters of thanks came pouring in – many so touching that Susannah felt obliged to publish some in *The Sword and the Trowel* to show the donors what relief and joy their gifts had brought:

Your great gift to me came safely to hand this morning. I cannot command language that will adequately convey to you the thanks I desire to offer. You will believe me when I say that the gift and the way in which it came to me, thoroughly broke me down, and tears of joy flowed freely. My salary is £60 a year and I have a wife and family . . .

SINGING IN THE FIRE

For the rest of her life Susannah Spurgeon toiled in the interest of the Book Fund. Often in weakness herself and increasingly called upon to care for Charles in his periods of illness and pain, she yet gave herself unreservedly to her self-appointed labour for the good of others. The number of volumes dispatched grew steadily until for some years Susannah supervised the distribution of ten thousand theological books a year. The service extended worldwide as Christian workers in many lands became grateful recipients of books from the Fund. By the time she was too frail and elderly to continue the work she could record a total of two hundred thousand books sent out to needy pastors. The correspondence, both in thanking donors and replying to queries, kept Susie at her post for many hours each day.

The Book Fund brought its own reward. Not only had Susie little time to brood on her own weakness and limitations, it also eased the pain of the long separations from Charles as he was obliged to spend each winter in the South of France to gain some relief from the crippling pain he so often endured. Susannah knew that pastors were eagerly awaiting the arrival of their parcels and if she failed they would be disappointed. Closely following the inauguration of the Book Fund came the 'Pastor's Aid Fund' – a natural development – for some of the letters revealed needs that Susannah dared not ignore. So gifts of money, clothing and toys accompanied the books, bringing relief and gladness into countless homes.

'If to make other people glad be a joy to your heart, then, dear Mrs Spurgeon, you ought to be a pre-eminently happy woman', wrote a grateful pastor, and this not long after the death of Charles in January 1892 – a loss which could well have broken Susie's spirit. So long had she now given herself in service to others with scant regard to her own needs, that she was able to continue her work unabated.

The Book Fund also led to the development of Susannah's literary gifts. Charles had encouraged and coaxed his retiring 'wifey', as he called her, into writing in the early days of their married life, but Susannah now had to write monthly reports on the progress of the Fund for *The Sword and the Trowel* magazine. Soon her own ability as a writer became apparent. Two autobiographical accounts of the work of the Book Fund, entitled *Ten Years of my Life in the Service of the Book Fund* (1886) and *Ten Years After* (1895) became popular reading. Other pamphlets, called the *Westwood Leaflets*, followed, and also three books of devotional readings with titles evocative in themselves, such as: *A Carillon of Bells to Ring Out the Old Truths of Free Grace and Dying Love* and *A Cluster of Camphire or Words of Comfort for Sick and Sorrowful Souls*.

The literary labour for which the Christian church has most cause for gratitude to Susannah Spurgeon is the editorial work which she carried out on her husband's autobiography. Charles had written this over a number of years and in a rather haphazard manner, for it was never a priority in his mind; so time and labour were needed to prepare it for publication. This Susannah willingly gave, together with Spurgeon's private secretary, Joseph Harrald. It was finally published in four ornate and sizeable volumes between 1897 and 1900. In keeping with her generation, Susannah's style could often be effusive, even sentimental, but purged of these defects, revised, and with some additions, her work has reappeared in modern form in the two-volume autobiography of Charles Haddon Spurgeon, entitled *The Early Years* and *The Full Harvest*, published in 1962 and 1973 respectively by the Banner of Truth Trust.

So it was that twelve years after the death of Charles,

Susie too, who had felt deeply the years of loneliness and separation, came to the end of her pilgrimage. In the summer of 1903 she was taken ill, but lingered on for many weeks. In early October it seemed the end was near and, addressing her son Thomas, she gave to both her sons a parting benediction: 'The double blessing of your father's God be upon you and your brother', she said. Some days later when very frail she was heard to whisper, 'Blessed Jesus! Blessed Jesus! I can see the King in his glory.' And on 22 October 1903, that vision became a reality for Susannah Spurgeon.

Archibald G. Brown, who had spoken to the vast throng congregated at her husband's graveside in 1892, also spoke the final words at Susannah's funeral. It was a sincere and moving tribute to a woman who had excelled, not only as the wife of a distinguished preacher, but also as an eminent example of Christian womanhood. 'Farewell, sister,' he concluded, 'we praise God for thee. For the help thou didst bring thy husband in his ceaseless toil and hard-fought battle, we are grateful. For thy ministry of love to the poor of our Lord's servants, hundreds of hearts enshrine thy memory . . . By faith we joy in thy joy, and triumph in thy final conquest . . . and humbly trust, through the blood of the everlasting covenant, to pass through the glory gates and know also "what it is to be there".'

Thomas Hog
Covenanter and Preacher

In prayer Thomas Hog was most solemn and fervent; the profoundest reverence, with the lowest submission and yet a marvellous boldness and intimacy with God. It might truly be said of him, as of Luther, that when he prayed it was with as much reverence as if he were speaking to God, and with as much boldness as if he had been speaking to his friend. The strength of his faith was proof against discouragement; none ever beheld him perplexed on account of difficulties. Having once committed his cause to the Lord, he could wait with assurance of a happy outcome.

MEMOIRS OF THOMAS HOG

5

Desolate, gaunt and windswept, the Bass Rock stands a perpetual memorial to the faith and endurance of the Scottish Covenanters of the seventeenth century. Little more than a third of a mile in diameter, the rock rises sheer above the choppy waters of the North Sea. On this rock stood a prison from which none could escape and here many a Covenanter languished, and some died, for conscience sake.

The Bass Rock, purchased by the crown in 1671 for the sum of £4,000, was to be used as a prison and it was ideally suited for such a purpose. Situated about two miles from the coast and adjacent to the Firth of Forth, it would conveniently accommodate prisoners brought from the Edinburgh courts. At one point alone could access be gained to this unwelcoming fortress and then only at high tide. The ruins of the old prison can still be seen in front and to the side of the lighthouse now standing on the Rock.

Thomas Hog was but one of the many Covenanters imprisoned on the Bass Rock. Here he suffered more than most, for at the special orders of Archbishop James Sharp, that Judas of the Scottish church, he was incarcerated in the lowest and darkest dungeon, being considered a greater threat than others to the king's intolerant religious strategy.

Born in 1628, the same year as John Bunyan, Thomas Hog was a Highland lad from Ross-shire. Over six feet tall and well-built, he soon gained respect, not merely for his physique, but for his academic ability. He studied well and then proceeded to the University of Aberdeen, graduating from there with a Master of Arts degree. Although Thomas had been born into a home where high moral standards were valued and the basic principles of religion carefully taught, he freely admits that throughout his early manhood he was a stranger to the grace of God. Outwardly all was correct: his sincerity, zeal, attendance at gatherings for prayer and worship, diligent study of the Scriptures and even his swift appeal to the throne of grace in times of need. But he himself knew that these things, commendable though they might be, were insufficient to save his soul while he lacked an inner convicting work of the Spirit.

On completing his student days, Thomas entered the service of the Earl of Sutherland in Dunrobin Castle, as one of his chaplains. During his period in this home he began to experience intense conviction of sin. 'His sins were set before him', his biographer informs us, 'with much of awful majesty, which produced amazement and deep abasement on his part.' So acute became the struggle in Thomas' soul that at times he was cast into despair. Satan took full advantage of this situation and on one occasion, as Thomas battled alone with his thoughts and the sense of the impending judgment of God for his sins, his eyes fell on a well-sharpened penknife lying on the table. Immediately Satan tempted him to self-destruction. Realising how weak he was in the face of this assault, he flung the penknife out of the open window. Like John Bunyan, and at nearly the same time, Hog gradually attained peace of soul and confidence in Christ as Saviour and Mediator and could declare himself 'willing through grace to forego, endure and in his strength adventure upon anything in his cause and for his sake.'

In 1654, at the age of twenty-six, Thomas Hog was called to become the minister in the Highland coastal parish of Kiltearn. On his arrival he found spiritual life at a low ebb. Many years had elapsed since the area last had a regular ministry and for the next eight years Hog laboured diligently: preaching, exhorting, visiting his people in their homes. Always self-effacing and reticent concerning his service for God, Hog has left little account of those remarkable days but from his successor we learn that soon 'the dry bones began to revive and pleasant blossoms and hopeful appearances displayed themselves everywhere through the parish.'

Though Thomas Hog and his wife Elizabeth were childless, the Lord had once consoled Thomas with the promise 'I will give you a name better than that of sons and daughters', and many were the children of grace born during Hog's ministry in Kiltearn. Amongst them was Katherine Collace, whose autobiography, written with meticulous care in her own hand, can still be seen. It bears testimony to the quality of ministry she enjoyed. Another notable convert was John Caird, a tinker by trade. He requested baptism for his child, but Hog courteously and kindly pointed out that John's own spiritual condition was far from satisfactory and he could not grant his request until John himself was different. The tinker was enraged at such a response from his pastor, but in the goodness of God his anger soon turned to deep sorrow for his sin. Rising early one Sunday morning, John Caird cried to God with urgency and importunity for forgiveness and mercy. The battle was fierce, but John dared not rest until he was assured of his acceptance with God. In exultation of spirit, he hurried to the church where he found Thomas Hog praying in private. 'O! Mr Thomas, Mr Thomas,' he interrupted, 'turn your prayers into praises on my account, for this day salvation has come to my soul.' John Caird lived to be nearly a hundred years of age, and all through his long life bore an exemplary testimony to the grace of God. One who met him at the end of his life described him as 'full of majesty and gravity'.

A quaint story has been recorded from those days. It tells of a relative of the Earl of Sutherland, Munro by name, whom Thomas Hog first met when he was in the Earl's service. Newly converted to God himself, Hog challenged Munro on the sinful course of his life demonstrated by his frivolous and godless conversation. Munro was convicted of his sin and soon became a changed man through the grace of God. Not long after Hog had settled at Kiltearn, Munro arrived at his door. After mutual greetings, Munro announced that God had given him a secret indication that his own life was drawing to a close and he would soon die. Munro, therefore, begged permission to spend his remaining days at Hog's house and under his ministry.

As his friend appeared to be in the best of health, Hog did his utmost to divert him from such gloomy premonitions. However, within a few days a violent fever overtook Munro, and he was clearly a dying man. Hog cared for him dutifully and on the Sunday made arrangements for him to be adequately nursed while Hog himself fulfilled his pulpit engagements. To his consternation, however, in the middle of his sermon, Hog suddenly noticed Munro sitting in the congregation. With some difficulty he finished the service and then hurried home. There he found the sick man lying in bed just as before. Hog demanded a reason for this bizarre behaviour and Munro explained: 'Sir, I had the first sermon that did me good from you . . . and I would get my last preaching from you also.' So, musing on the sermon he had so recently heard, Munro died, and in the very circumstances he had requested.

A number of anecdotes have survived, some quite remarkable, that illustrate unusual and significant answers to prayer given to Thomas Hog both during his period at Kiltearn and also later in life. There are also some records that appear to demonstrate a strange foreknowledge of future events: one or two well-documented accounts must suffice as examples of this. When Hog was preaching on one occasion at the Laird of Lethem's home he noticed one of the servants continually laughing during the service. The first rebuke Hog gave was gentle, but when the man continued laughing, heedless of the admonition, Hog was more severe in his reproof. But all to no avail. The merriment and disdain for the preached word continued. At last Hog paused and then proclaimed with dramatic severity, 'The Spirit of God is grieved at one of the company for mocking at these great truths: therefore I am bold to say . . . that such offers of grace shall be visibly and more suddenly punished than any here would wish and that the guilty person would give much for our prayers when he cannot have them.' That very night the man was struck with a violent illness and called for Hog, but though Hog hurried to him without a moment's delay, the man was dead before he could reach him.

Perhaps the most notable instance of Thomas Hog's sense of future events was demonstrated in his farewell sermon to his parishioners after he was ejected from his pulpit in Kiltearn in 1662. Eight years had passed since Hog had begun his work in the town – years in which he had witnessed a spiritual transformation among the people as God had blessed his endeavours. And now, following the Restoration of Charles II to the throne in 1660, legislation had been passed requiring all ministers installed in churches since 1649 to regularise their position by applying to the bishops. Thomas Hog and over four hundred other Scottish ministers had no liberty of conscience to do this. These men chose eviction, poverty, banishment and even death rather than the path of compromise.

A sorrowful congregation assembled to hear their pastor's last admonitions. But it was in these circumstances that Hog made a bold prediction which he also coupled with a solemn warning. Dark storm clouds were gathering over Scotland and his own prospects appeared precarious but, looking far on into the future, Hog declared that though the storm would be of long duration, the skies would eventually clear. More than this, he assured his hearers that he himself would live to see that day and would be restored to his beloved church once more to die among them in that place. Then he added this grave caution: 'If any of you shall decline from that good way, and these truths wherein you have been taught, and shall comply with the wicked designs now carried on, I take heaven and earth to be witnesses against you; I take the stones of these walls I preach in, every word that was spoken, and every one of you to be witnesses against another.'

Thomas Hog was right. The storm was protracted over three decades and many good men suffered and died before the skies cleared again. Thomas Hog was thirty-four years of age when he was evicted from his church and home, and it was not until he was sixty-three that he eventually saw the fulfilment of his prediction.

During the first few years after his ejection from Kiltearn, Thomas Hog and Elizabeth his wife went to Knockgoudy in Morayshire, where Elizabeth's brother owned property. Although banned from public preaching, Hog exercised a ministry from this home and many were the men and women, deprived of the means of grace, who found their way to Knockgoudy. Moved by the spiritual needs of the people, Hog was emboldened to conduct a public communion service in 1668. The risk was great and Hog paid a heavy price for his courage. He was arrested and imprisoned. Katherine Collace, who appears to have followed Hog from Kiltearn, reports on a gathering for prayer on Hog's behalf. In answer to the supplications of his people and against all natural expectations, God intervened and Hog was soon set at liberty once more.

Although Thomas Hog was not in sympathy with the more extreme methods adopted by some Covenanters in their struggle for religious independence, he was resolute in his stand for the truth and in opposition to the interference by the state in the life and worship of Christ's church. In 1676 he was arrested again and for the same offence. Declaring, 'I trust in the living God, and before my conscience shall get a scratch, this neck shall go for it', Hog was hustled off for another period of imprisonment. This time it was on the Bass Rock.

When Thomas Hog arrived at his desolate and inclement prison, he found at least one consolation: other men with whom he could share spiritual fellowship were already there. Alexander Peden, that romantic and colourful figure of the Scottish Covenanting era, was among them. 'Puir auld Sandy' had already spent two and a half years on the Bass Rock when Hog arrived and would remain there for a further eighteen months. John McGilligen of Fodderty and Thomas Ross of Tain were also his fellow sufferers. When James Fraser of Brea, Hog's close friend and colleague of former years, joined them in 1677, it was an added compensation.

The conditions on the Bass Rock have been described in vivid detail by James Fraser in his *Memoirs*. Sometimes the deafening roar of wind and sea reverberating around the Rock would overawe the men. The waves, frequently over thirty feet in height, would dash right over the prison walls. Rations were meagre, often consisting of dry fish and oatmeal. Drinking water was contaminated: in summer it was taken from rain water preserved in rock pools and in winter from melted snow. Usually the prisoners were free to converse and mix with one another, but at times even this joy was removed by some officious prison warden who would split them up and demand silence. A little exercise was allowed occasionally and then the prisoners would be conducted two by two to the top of the Rock and back again, the distance of about half a mile.

It was little wonder that under such circumstances Thomas Hog soon became ill, developing the alarming symptoms of tuberculosis. His condition deteriorated rapidly and a doctor from Edinburgh had to be summoned. Noting the gravity of his state, the doctor said he could hold out little hope of life unless Hog was released immediately to recuperate in better conditions. Hog was reluctant to plead with Archbishop Sharp for clemency. Probably he knew he would receive none. So concerned was the doctor over his patient's condition, however, that he put in a personal plea before the Archbishop and his council, meeting all the clerical costs of the hearing himself.

When the request was read out many council members urged Sharp to show mercy, explaining that Thomas Hog was more restrained in his opposition to the policies of the regime than others. But Archbishop Sharp was adamant. He maintained that Hog could do more damage to their cause seated in his armchair than twenty others could do travelling up and down the kingdom. No, he insisted. If divine retribution were calling Mr Hog off this earthly stage, it would be wrong of him to intervene and prevent such justice from taking its course. If there were any worse place in the Bass Rock prison than the one in which

Hog was currently being held he should be moved to it immediately. 'The closest prison in the Bass for him', declared the heartless Archbishop.

When Thomas Hog received the sentence, he was so ill that he could scarcely sit up in his bed to read it. Then he merely remarked that it was as severe as if Satan himself had penned it. As Hog was carried down to the low, damp underground dungeon, his friends wept openly. 'Now,' exclaimed one, 'your death is unavoidable.' But Hog seemed unusually calm. 'Now that men have no mercy,' he explained, 'the Lord will show himself merciful. The moment I enter this dungeon I will begin to recover.' And so he did. Ever after when he heard Archbishop Sharp's name mentioned, he would say cheerfully, 'Recommend him for me as a good physician!'

Later in 1677 it appears that Thomas Hog was removed from the Bass Rock and taken to the Edinburgh Tolbooth, and in October of that year he was sent to Kintyre where a heavy fine was threatened if he should attempt to escape. It is difficult to trace his movements during the next five years but clearly neither imprisonment nor fines could silence this intrepid preacher. In 1683 we find him arrested once more and charged with 'holding private conventicles' or preaching and ministering God's word despite the public ban and dire penalties imposed on men and women caught either attending or officiating at such outlawed gatherings. This time he was banished from Scotland and ordered to leave the country within forty-eight hours or face an exorbitant fine.

There seemed no alternative but to emigrate to the Continent. So Hog made his way to London, but before long found himself in prison yet again and under straitened circumstances. Merely on the rumour of a plot against the king – a plot in which he had no part – Hog was apprehended, for he was clearly a marked man. In

1686 Thomas and Elizabeth Hog finally left their native shores for Holland, with little prospect of return in human terms.

The storm had indeed been long and sharp, but the skies were soon to clear, and in 1688 came the 'Glorious Revolution' when William of Orange sailed from Holland together with Mary his wife, to take the throne of England and James II fled for his life. Thomas and Elizabeth gladly returned to Scotland that same year. Broken and worn with the years of suffering and privation, Thomas had not long to live. But in 1691 he returned to his people in Kiltearn as he had predicted nearly thirty years earlier.

Thomas Hog died well, though the end was hard and accompanied by much pain. Once when his servant heard him groaning, he enquired whether it was pain of body or of soul that extorted from him such deep groans. 'No soul-trouble, man,' Hog replied, 'for a hundred and a hundred times my Lord has assured me that I shall be with him for ever, but I am making moan for my body.' He longed for the day of deliverance from his pain-racked condition. 'Pity me, O my friends, and do not pray for my life', he exclaimed. 'Allow me to go to my eternal rest.'

As the end drew near, the light of heaven grew more intense. 'Never did the sun shine more brightly . . . than Christ, the Sun of Righteousness, hath shined on my soul', Hog confessed. 'The unchangeableness of God is my rock,' he maintained, when low through weakness and pain. Thomas Hog had often spoken of the day when Christ his Lord would come, and in his dying the longing of years was fulfilled. 'Now he is come, he is come, my Lord is come! Praises, praises to him for evermore', he exclaimed. And with these words this noble and suffering Covenanter entered the world of light. Even in death Thomas Hog still spoke a message of warning to the parishioners of Kiltearn, for he was buried across the threshold of the church and this inscription was placed on his gravestone:

THIS STONE SHALL BEAR WITNESS
AGAINST THE PARISHIONERS OF KILTEARN
IF THEY BRING ANE UNGODLY MINISTER
IN HERE.

MONICA
The Conversion of Augustine

Narrow is the mansion of my soul; enlarge thou it, that thou mayest enter in. It is ruinous; repair thou it. It has that within which must offend thine eyes; I confess and know it. But who shall cleanse it, or to whom should I cry, save thee? Lord, cleanse me from my secret faults, and spare thy servant from the power of the enemy.

AUGUSTINE'S PRAYER

6

A young teenager was kicking a ball around. He had a keen competitive spirit and found that the attractions of a game with his friends frequently lured him from his schoolwork despite threats and punishments from parents and teachers alike. The description sounds contemporary – but the schoolboy lived more than sixteen hundred years ago. He was none other than the young Augustine, one day to become the renowned Augustine of Hippo.

Augustine was born in Tagaste, a small provincial town in North Africa, now called Souk-Ahras, in modern Algeria. His mother, Monica, was a woman of eminent Christian faith and piety, while his pagan father, Patricius, was a churlish and unattractive character. When Augustine was born in A.D. 354, Monica was twenty-three years of age and from earliest days she surrounded her infant son with her prayers and taught him about Christ. Young Augustine gave early evidence of an exceptional mind and both his parents were eager for his academic success. But highly intelligent though he was, even the lash of his schoolmaster's whip failed to drive Augustine to his studies and 'by innumerable lies' he discovered ways of evading any work which he found irksome.

Despite his disinclination to study, Augustine's obvious ability led Monica and Patricius to direct their son towards a legal career. They planned to send him to Carthage when he was seventeen to begin his training. But as this would involve heavy expense, throughout the previous year they withdrew Augustine from school, while they tried to raise the necessary finance. Augustine's year of enforced idleness proved to be the young man's undoing. Out of sheer boredom he committed acts of petty theft for the mere enjoyment of the escapade. When he heard his peers bragging about their lawless behaviour, he would invent degrading sins which he had not committed and would boast of them in order to impress his companions.

Christian literature has been profoundly enriched by the spiritual autobiographies of men and women of faith across the centuries. *The Confessions of St. Augustine* is one of the earliest and most influential accounts of the grace of God to a man ever set on record. With disarming honesty Augustine traces his life from infancy through to manhood. Passionate and excitable by nature, Augustine fully admits his sensual and immoral ways and the tortuous path of unbelief he followed until his eventual conversion at the age of thirty-two. But interwoven throughout the narrative like a shining thread, runs a parallel account, as moving and encouraging as the former is grievous. It is the account of the prayers and faith of his mother, Monica, and of God's dealings with her, as he gave her courage and strength to persevere in her entreaties.

During Augustine's year of idleness, he embarked on that life of immorality which so marred his unregenerate years. 'The briers of unclean desires grew rank over my head', Augustine acknowledged sadly in his *Confessions*, 'and there was no hand to root them out.' While Patricius showed little concern over his son's behaviour, Monica was startled and troubled. She warned him repeatedly of the end of such a way of life, but all to no avail. Yet God was not indifferent. It is of this period of his life that Augustine was to write:

I escaped not thy scourges, for what mortal can? For thou wast ever with me, mercifully rigorous and besprinkling with most bitter alloy all my unlawful pleasure, that I might seek pleasure without alloy. But where to find such, I could not discover, save in thee, O Lord, who teachest by sorrow, and woundest us to heal, and killest us, lest we die from thee.

After this regrettable year, Augustine went to Carthage. Here he studied well; but his father died shortly after his arrival, leaving the future of his studies in doubt. A friend, Romanius, noting his abilities, kindly financed the remainder of his training, enabling Augustine to continue in Carthage. But his abandoned way of life continued: the racecourse, the amphitheatre and gambling houses of Carthage led the young man further astray. His own comment on his way of life during these days is revealing: 'I was foul, and dishonourable', he admits. It may well be that Augustine was not so very different from other young men, for these bitter self-accusations were made after his conscience was enlightened with the knowledge of God's holy standards.

During Augustine's studies he came across a work by Cicero which turned his sensual mind towards nobler ideals. 'How did I burn, O my God, how did I burn to remount from earthly things to thee', he declares. He began to study the Scriptures, but his darkened mind failed to grasp the truth and before long he abandoned this study, turning aside to a heresy called Manichaeanism.

From the age of nineteen and for nine years, Augustine was caught in the net of this philosophical and superstitious system of thought. It was a confused mixture of aspects of Christianity and Persian religion which set as its aim the release of the purified soul from the prison house of its material body. Monica was heartbroken that he should be entangled in such a snare. Many were the secret tears and prayers she offered to God on behalf of her erring son. Looking back on those days, Augustine describes his mother's sorrow:

My mother, thy faithful one, wept to thee for me, more than mothers weep the bodily deaths of their children. For she, by that faith and spirit which she had from thee, discerned the death wherein I lay, and thou heardest her, O Lord, and didst not despise her tears, when streaming down, they watered the ground in every place where she prayed.

To comfort Monica, God spoke to her by means of a dream assuring her that one day Augustine would be converted. In her dream she saw a shining youth approaching her. He asked her why she was grieving, and Monica replied that her tears were due to her son's lost condition. At this the shining youth gave her an assurance that one day Augustine would be where she was. But when she repeated her dream to Augustine, he perversely turned the meaning round, informing his mother that it indicated that one day she would be where he was.

During the whole of this period Augustine was living with a woman to whom he was not married and a son, Adeodatus, was born from this relationship. Always Monica followed Augustine with her prayers, though at times it seemed as if he grew more heedless and hardened in unbelief. But never did Monica cease to believe that one day she would receive an answer to her supplications. Sometimes she was tempted to despair, but always she clung to the hope born in her heart from the dream she had received.

'For almost nine years', says Augustine, 'I wallowed in the mire of that deep pit [Manichaeanism], and the darkness of falsehood . . . all which time that chaste, godly widow, now more cheered with hope, yet not one whit relaxing in her weeping and mourning, ceased not to bewail my case unto thee. And yet thou sufferest me to be yet involved and reinvolved in that darkness.' Unable by any arguments of her own to reason further with Augustine or dissuade him from his follies, Monica thought of another expedient. Perhaps the local bishop, well-versed as he was in biblical truth, might speak to her son. When she approached him with her request, he declined, saying that Augustine was still unteachable, being puffed up with his supposed knowledge. But the bishop was a wise man and his advice brought consolation to Monica – and also to many other praying parents who have read his words since that day. 'Let him alone a while, only pray God for him . . . Go thy ways and God bless thee, for it is not possible that the son of these tears should perish.'

At last, when Augustine was twenty-seven years of age, he began to be delivered from the Manichaean error by observing the corrupt lives of some of its adherents who claimed to have attained to high standards of purity. By this time Augustine had returned to his home town of Tagaste, and was engaged as a teacher of grammar. But after the death of a close friend he was so distressed that he felt he must move from the scenes they had shared, so he returned to Carthage. Here he began to lecture in the art of rhetoric. Here too he met the leader of the Manichaean sect, Faustus. Augustine was quickly able to detect his hypocrisy and this added to his disillusionment with the heresy. His students in Carthage proved a rude and indisciplined group and so Augustine decided he would sail for Rome.

But he had reckoned without Monica. She feared that in Rome her wayward son would be beyond all influence of Christianity and so begged him with many tears to remain in Carthage. Augustine, however, was determined and he stooped to the unworthy trick of lying to his mother, then sailed for Rome before she realised he had gone.

When Monica discovered that the ship had sailed she was 'frantic with sorrow' and 'with complaints and groans' pleaded with God that the ship might return. Yet God was answering her prayers at the very moment that she felt her petitions were most rejected. For, as Augustine later commented, 'Thou in the depth of Thy counsels regardest not what she then asked, that Thou mightest make me what she ever asked.' Augustine records also that his mother's grief at his departure was not wholly spiritual, but sprang in part from a human devotion which could not endure to be parted from him. So, he comments, 'the earthly part of her affection to me was punished by the allotted scourge of sorrows.'

Disappointed by the unscrupulous behaviour of his students in Rome also, Augustine soon moved on to Milan. Here it was that God himself intended to apprehend and convert this man through the influence of Ambrose, who was then Bishop of Milan. 'I was led to him unknowingly by God that I might be led knowingly to God by him', Augustine wrote in his *Confessions*. Throughout the following two years, Augustine slowly cast off the lingering effects of the Manichaean heresy and listened earnestly to the preaching of Ambrose.

Monica, meanwhile, had taken ship and followed her son to Milan, solicitous as ever of his spiritual welfare. Gradually Augustine became convinced of the truths that Ambrose preached. Only one obstacle remained: the problem of his lust. Augustine feared the cost of following Christ. His cry was, 'Give me chastity, but not yet.' He decided it would be better if he became married, but strangely, he dismissed the woman with whom he had lived so long and whom he loved, choosing instead a girl who was not yet of marriageable age. While waiting for her to come of age, he tells us that he formed yet another illicit relationship.

But a crisis was fast approaching. Now Augustine was giving himself to constant study of the Scriptures and despite his continued sinful way of life and philosophical arguments, spiritual light began to penetrate his soul. The experience of the Apostle Paul matched his own, for though he now delighted in the law of God after the inner man, he too found another law at work in his members bringing him into captivity until, like the Apostle, he could cry out, 'O wretched man that I am.'

An account of a notable scholar, who had also lectured in rhetoric in Rome and had faced the ridicule of his intellectual colleagues when he was converted, moved Augustine profoundly. He began at last to see himself in the light of God's purity and the sight appalled him. 'How foul I was, how crooked and defiled', he exclaimed.

The struggle came to a climax as Augustine and a friend, Alypius, with whom he shared accommodation, listened to yet another account of a man who had given up all for Christ. As he listened, Augustine's inward agitation of spirit became unbearable. 'What ails us, Alypius?' he demanded, in a voice that betrayed the depth of his emotion. 'Are we ashamed to follow?' With these words he rushed out into the garden, closely followed by Alypius. There he sat, the intensity of the struggle affecting his whole face and body. At last he rose, left Alypius, and went to the farthest corner of the garden. Here he flung himself down under a tree and wept like a child: 'How long, O Lord? Wilt Thou be angry for ever? Remember not our former iniquities', he pleaded.

It was at that moment that he heard what seemed like a child's clear voice chanting over and over again, 'Take up and read. Take up and read.' To the distressed man it came as a divine instruction. He rose, went back to

Alypius, and picked up the Scriptures he had left open on the ground. The words on which his eyes fell were these: '. . . not in revelry and drunkenness, not in licentiousness and lewdness, . . . But put on the Lord Jesus Christ, and make no provision for the flesh, to fulfil its lusts' (*Rom.* 13:13–14). 'Instantly', he tells us, 'by a light as it were of serenity infused into my heart, all the darkness of doubt vanished away.' Of that moment he was to write: 'How sweet it did at once become to me to be without those toys [his immoral ways], and what I feared to lose, I now rejoiced to cast away.'

Speedily Augustine and his friend, Alypius, also converted on that same day, went to share the news with Monica, whose joys were the greater because of the depths of anxiety she had known and the intensity of her prolonged intercession. Before long both Augustine and Alypius were baptized, together with Adeodatus, Augustine's son, now fifteen years of age, whom Augustine describes as 'a contemporary in grace'.

Soon after this, Augustine completed his period as Professor of Rhetoric in Milan; nothing more remained but for him to return to North Africa, and so, with his mother and son, he set sail; Monica was then fifty-six and Augustine thirty-three years of age. Breaking their journey at Ostia, a quiet coastal town, Augustine records in detail a conversation he had with his mother there. Unknown to either of them, Monica's life was drawing swiftly to a close. Together they stood at an open window, looking out onto a quiet garden, and began to speak of the joys that await believers in the eternal world. So delightful was their conversation that Augustine records, 'We gasped after those heavenly streams of thy fountain, the fountain of life.' Time itself seemed to fall away: 'Hushed were the images of earth and waters and air.' It seemed they were almost in heaven while still on earth

'This world with all its delights became contemptible to us', wrote Augustine. At that moment Monica turned and said to Augustine:

Son, for my own part I have no further delight in anything in this life. What I do here any longer, and to what end I am here, I know not, now that my hopes in this world are accomplished. One thing there was for which I desired to linger for a while in this life, that I might see you a Christian before I died . . .

Five days later Monica was taken ill, and died after an illness of nine days' duration. Asked if she were afraid to die so far from home, she replied, 'Nothing is far from God.' She did not live to see her son become Bishop of Hippo, nor did she know that he would be a valiant champion for truth against encroaching heresies, or that he would be esteemed greatest among the early Church Fathers. Enough it was for Monica that her son had been converted by the grace of God in answer to her earnest supplications.

MARGARET BAXTER
A Puritan Romance

My whole, though broken heart, O Lord,
From henceforth shall be thine!
And here I do my vows record:
This hand, these words, are mine.
All that I have without reserve
I offer here to thee:
Thy will and honour all shall serve,
All first bestowed on me.

Christ leads me through no darker rooms
Than he went through before,
And he that to God's kingdom comes
Must enter by this door.
Come, Lord, when grace has made me meet,
Thy blessed face to see:
For if thy work on earth be sweet,
What will thy glory be?

RICHARD BAXTER
Based on the covenant signed by Margaret Baxter
after her illness, 1660

7

In 1681 Richard Baxter, eminent Puritan preacher, took up his pen to write a short account of the life of his wife, Margaret. It was written, as he freely confessed, 'under the power of a melting grief', for only six weeks earlier God had 'called away to his blessed rest and glory, the spirit of the most dear companion of the last nineteen years of my life.'

It had been a particularly happy marriage. 'We lived in inviolated love,' declared Baxter, 'and I know not that we ever had any breach in the point of love or the point of interest, save only that she somewhat grudged that I had persuaded her, for my quietness, to surrender so much of her estate, to a disabling her from helping others so much as she earnestly desired.' Yet the circumstances of their married life were far from easy. Never were they to know a settled home life for any length of time: wherever her persecuted husband was driven, Margaret followed. When he was put into prison for his refusal to comply with the arbitrary demands of the corrupt Restoration government, she accompanied him there. 'She brought her best bed thither and did much to remove the inconveniences of the prison', Richard commented.

Under the shadow of The Wrekin in Shropshire and less than a mile from Wellington, Margaret Charlton was born at Apley Castle in 1636. Her father, Francis Charlton, came from an old and highly respected family, but died in 1642 when his three children were scarcely old enough to remember him. His death left his widow,

Mary, highly vulnerable for in that same year the Civil War broke out. With the family's strong Royalist sympathies, it was not long before Apley Castle was stormed by the Parliamentary forces. Shortly after this, Margaret's mother remarried and Thomas Hanmer, her second husband, ordered all the family servants and tenants on the estate to arm against further attack.

In 1644, however, the castle came under siege once more, and this time was plundered and used as a soldiers' garrison. It was a traumatic experience for the eight-year-old Margaret and one she could never forget. Her stepfather was taken prisoner, and died shortly afterwards; part of the castle was set alight, some lay dead, while Margaret herself and many others were left, stripped of clothing and helpless.

By some unknown means Margaret's mother managed to smuggle her three young children from the scene of danger and also away from an uncle who wished to take over their guardianship, probably from ulterior motives. They found refuge in an Essex village until the hostilities were over but as soon as it was safe they returned to Apley Castle. Mary Hanmer, clearly a practical and capable woman, supervised repair work on the property and managed the estate until her son, the youngest of her children, was old enough to undertake the responsibility.

In 1657 Margaret's mother decided to leave the castle and move to Kidderminster. Here it was that Richard Baxter had ministered since 1641, apart from the years of the Civil War, and during that period had witnessed an astonishing spiritual transformation in the town, by the help of God. Apley Castle was only twenty miles away, and Mary Hanmer had undoubtedly heard reports of the changes at Kidderminster and was anxious to benefit from such a ministry herself. Her first contact with Richard Baxter, however, was unpromising. He strongly advised her against the move, feeling that her duty lay in giving moral support to her son at the castle. But she disregarded his advice and arrived in the town secretly, taking rented accommodation. The following year, Margaret, who had been staying with her older sister in Oxford, joined her mother.

Nothing about Margaret Charlton could have suggested, even to the most discerning eye, that here was a potential life-partner for the renowned other-worldly preacher. Baxter was forty-three, and known to favour celibacy in the ministry; Margaret was an attractive, though slightly giddy-headed young woman of twenty-two. Fond of frivolous company and with a flair for expensive, fashionable clothes, Margaret had little room for serious or contemplative thought. With her spirited and romantic turn of mind, she imagined that religion could only deprive her of her pleasures.

Life in Kidderminster did not appeal to Margaret. Accustomed to the cheerful freedom of her days in Oxford, she regarded her new acquaintances as strict and their way of life drab and uninteresting. Nothing but affection for her mother had induced Margaret to come, but as she sat under Baxter's preaching her attitudes began to change. At first she admitted she was 'not as she should be', and then that 'something better should be attained'. Baxter's preaching was ardent and searching and as Margaret listened it 'was received on her heart as the seal on the wax'. Clearly the Spirit of God was at work in this worldly-minded girl.

Now Margaret no longer listened to the preaching in a detached manner but with deepening concern, even anxiety. She became serious in her life-view and her behaviour changed markedly. A maid who worked for Margaret's mother noticed how frequently the young woman slipped into her bedroom for secret prayer and she could often be overheard pleading earnestly for the salvation of her soul. A strong awareness of sin dominated her thinking at this time and a paper discovered after her death reveals the depth of conviction which she experienced. Responding to a sermon of Baxter's on the importance of self-examination, Margaret is ruthless in her analysis of her own heart condition. 'Christ's Spirit inclineth to love, humility and meekness', Baxter had pointed out. 'None more uncharitable, proud and censorious than I', Margaret acknowledged. 'My self-conceitedness shows that I am unhumbled.'

Richard Baxter was a masterly physician of souls as his work, *The Reformed Pastor*, first published in 1657 and still widely read today, amply demonstrates. Well aware though he was of Margaret's spiritual struggle, he did not hurry to reassure her that all was well but records, 'these convictions did not die, nor yet pass into despair, but to serious conversion.' After some months of inner conflict, and quite suddenly it would appear, Margaret was brought into spiritual peace. 'God seemed sharply to entertain this returning soul', Baxter concludes.

Widespread joy at the conversion of the young woman so recently come to Kidderminster soon turned to anxiety, however, for Margaret, who had never been physically strong, fell seriously ill. Her condition, (she had probably contracted tuberculosis) deteriorated rapidly, until she was apparently dying. Baxter, sharing in the general concern, grieved that 'such a changed person should presently be taken away before she had time to manifest her sincerity or do God any service in the world'. He called the church to prayer and fasting for her recovery. 'Compassion made us extraordinarily fervent', he commented. In addition he recommended some of his own celebrated medical remedies, but admits that these did not contribute to Margaret's return to health. 'God

heard us and speedily delivered her as it were by nothing
or by an altogether undesigned means.'

Margaret's recovery began in December 1659 and by
April the following year a special service was held to give
thanks to God for so significant an answer to the prayers
of the church. Aware that God had intervened remarkably
in the course of her illness and saved her from an early
death, Margaret was anxious to fulfil the vows she had
made in her sickness and use this opportunity as a time of
self-dedication. Baxter asked her to suggest anything for
which she would especially wish them to give thanks. So
Margaret compiled a list of God's mercies towards her
and accompanied it with a solemn covenant of devotion
to God. Baxter was later to compose some verses based
on Margaret's words which she signed as a true expression
of her desires:

> *Lord, it belongs not to my care*
> *Whether I die or live,*
> *To love and serve thee is my share,*
> *And this thy grace must give.*
>
> *If life be long I will be glad*
> *That I may long obey;*
> *If short, then why should I be sad*
> *To soar to endless day?*

These lines form the opening verses of a hymn which
can still be found in most English hymnals. Long after the
service was over, and late into the night, Margaret sat
up recording her further contemplations and spiritual
aspirations. These she kept secret and Baxter only discovered them after her death. Some of her words are so
similar to Baxter's own in his work *The Saints' Everlasting
Rest*, published in 1650, that it suggests that Margaret
probably knew long passages by heart. Oblivious of time,

she sat writing – page after page: her desires after humility, her fear of sin, her acquiescence in God's providential ways towards her, and her wish to serve her God more faithfully.

But Margaret was troubled. Gnawing at her heart she discovered a growing affection for her pastor and spiritual guide, Richard Baxter. It was an affection stronger than she dared admit. Not only was it a love she could never hope to see returned, but it appeared to her to be in competition with her newly-awakened love to God – it was a 'creature-comfort' and she struggled to suppress it. 'Why should my heart be fixed where my home is not?' Margaret demanded of herself:

Heaven is my home; God in Christ is all my happiness . . . Come away, O my heart, from vanity; mount heavenward. Hath not experience taught thee that creature-comforts, though they may be roses, have their pricks? . . . Away then, O my carnal heart! retire to God, the only satisfying object. There mayest thou love without all danger of excess. Let thy love to God be fixed and transcendent. Amen.

To add to Margaret's disquiet, Richard Baxter was shortly due to leave Kidderminster for London. These were momentous times: Oliver Cromwell's death in 1658 had left a leadership vacuum in the nation which his son was unable to fill. A strong move was afoot to invite Charles I's son back from his exile to occupy the throne. Richard Baxter's writings and influence had set him among the foremost churchmen in the land and his support was eagerly sought for any such decision. The Earl of Lauderdale had expressed a desire to confer with him over the issue, hoping to eliminate the basic distrust Baxter felt concerning Charles. So it was that Baxter planned to journey to London. Here he was shortly to play a significant role in the recall of Charles II and

contrary to his expectations, future events were to pre-
clude any resumption of his ministry in Kidderminster.

Did Margaret sense these things? Certainly she felt
keenly the prospect of parting. Would they ever meet
again? Had she squandered her opportunities of profiting
from his ministry? 'I have now cause of sorrow,' she
recorded, 'for parting with my dear friend, my father, my
pastor . . . What the Lord will do with him I cannot
foresee.' Her consolation lay in looking away from earthly
scenes to a day when 'friends shall meet and never part
and remember their sad and weary days and nights no
more. Then farewell sorrow! farewell hard heart! farewell
tears and sad repentance!' So Margaret sat writing down
her thoughts as fast as they poured from her mind.
Suddenly she realised it was 'twelve of the clock'. She
must conclude her meditations and so wrote, 'No matter
if I had no friend near me and none on earth; if God
be not far from me it is well enough . . . Presently the
storm will be all over. Let me therefore cast all my care on
God.'

Even though Margaret strove to bring her affections
under control and grieved over the forthcoming separation, such was the strength of her attachment that she
was already planning, if at all possible, to follow Baxter to
London. 'I resolve, if Providence concur, to go to London
as soon as I can after the day of thanksgiving', she wrote.

Some have speculated over whether Baxter himself was
aware of Margaret's affection at this juncture. Most
probably he had indeed guessed her secret. Between the
paragraphs which she herself wrote that night, Margaret
transcribed excerpts from Baxter's letters giving pastoral
advice to the young convert. It would appear that his
words were designed to quench the ardour of the flame so
clearly burning in Margaret's heart. 'Too strong love to
any, though it be good in the kind, may be sinful and

hurtful in the degree. It will turn too many of your thoughts from God, and they will be too oft running after the beloved creature', he admonishes; and again: 'The best creature-affections have a mixture of creature-imperfections, and therefore need some gall to wean us from the faulty part . . . Learn by experience, when any condition is inordinately or excessively sweet to thee, to say, "from hence must be my sorrow".' And after these words Margaret adds in brackets, 'O how true!' Though Margaret's love for her mother was deep and sincere, such words could scarcely be applied to that relationship.

Did Baxter feel any kindred emotion towards Margaret? We cannot know. Certainly he mentions that there were 'other reasons' for his removal to London and the authority with which he seeks to dissuade her from her proposed visit suggests that he may well have been conscious of his own vulnerability in this respect and was determined to eradicate any affection he might have felt. The discrepancy in their ages was an important factor in his thinking; also his 'former known purposes against marriage and against the conveniency of ministers' marriage' added to his difficulties. More than this, the disparity between their social positions would be a further obstacle. Margaret was of aristocratic birth and an heiress to considerable wealth, while Richard was from a modest family background and could boast few material resources.

'It is not lawful to speak an idle word and especially deliberately; much less to go on an idle journey,' Baxter had remonstrated. But Margaret was determined on such 'an idle journey' and to London she went, together with her mother, not many weeks after Baxter himself had left. Perhaps Margaret had confided her affection to her mother. Certainly they both missed his preaching. Together they rented apartments in Sweeting's Alley (now Aldersgate Street).

Shortly after his arrival in London, Baxter, whose health was a cause of constant anxiety, faced a period of illness. In addition, his accommodation was unsettled and his preaching was quickly censured by his opponents. In such circumstances we can readily believe that the presence of Margaret and her mother so near at hand must have been a consolation to him. At first Baxter remained hopeful of his new king who had sent a message from Breda, his place of exile, promising: '. . . liberty to tender consciences and that no man shall be disquieted or called into question for differences of opinion on matters of religion.' But Baxter's early reservations were confirmed and, like many others, he was sadly disappointed as the true character of Charles II became manifest. No sooner had the king ascertained that no party was in a strong enough position to oppose him than he reneged on all his pledges. Baxter, who had been appointed a royal chaplain, attended the Savoy Conference, ostensibly convened so that the moderate Puritan party, whose views Baxter represented, could propose amendments to the Book of Common Prayer. But it was a farce: the king was only playing for time. Gradually Baxter came to see and fear the shape of things to come under the monarch he himself had helped to recall. When he was offered the bishopric of Hereford he refused it, knowing well the compromise that such a position would inevitably entail. He wished to return to Kidderminster but by the manoeuvrings of the previous vicar, influenced and controlled by one of his former parishioners, a wealthy old man who had once been a courtier, this opportunity was denied him, much against the wishes of the people.

Amid all the uncertainties of those days, of this Richard Baxter could be confident: there was one home where he could always be sure of a sympathetic hearing and one refuge at least from the storm of criticism he so often endured. In writing of the way in which his eventual marriage to Margaret Charlton came about, Baxter speaks of 'many strange occurrences which brought it to pass.' One of these must surely have been the unexpected death of Margaret's mother, Mary Hanmer, in January 1661. Mrs Hanmer had been a woman of remarkable gifts coupled with that godliness and spiritual zeal which has for ever distinguished the Puritan character. It was a crushing sorrow for Margaret who had loved her mother devotedly. Now she was left: a stranger in a strange city. To whom could she turn for advice and consolation? Surely it would be to Richard Baxter. Gradually their names became increasingly linked together as it became evident that an affection deeper than mere pastoral concern bound them the one to the other.

And of course the gossips soon had plenty to engage their tongues. Their friendship became 'a matter of much public talk and wonder' and Baxter comments with a blend of wry humour and exasperation, 'It everywhere rung about, partly as a wonder and partly as a crime . . . and I think the king's marriage was scarce more talked of than mine.' The Lord Chancellor had even heard a rumour that they were already married fully a year before it happened!

Throughout 1661 Baxter preached to crowded congregations, two or three times during the week and also on each Sunday. But the times were growing darker. John Bunyan was already in prison and in June of that year James Guthrie, prominent Scottish church leader, endured a martyr's death at the Grassmarket in Edinburgh. In May 1662 came at last the Act of Uniformity which required all preachers to swear by oath that they would conform to all the regulations of the Book of Common Prayer within three months or face expulsion from their livings and a ban on any further preaching. This was no mere quibble over words, phrases or church order; rather the Act, calling for 'unfeigned assent and consent' to all that was in the Prayer Book, carried at its heart a repudiation of the gospel itself.

Then dawned Black Bartholomew's Day: 24 August 1662. This was the day the Act came into force – a watershed in the history of the English church. Two thousand of England's best men were cast out of their churches and schools, often to penury and homelessness. 'I lay in tears, in deepest sorrow', wrote Baxter. Nor were his tears merely on account of his own deprivation, but they were for the travail of the true Church of Jesus Christ and the demise of all his aspirations for church unity.

But his sorrows were not without consolation. Now 'at last' and 'after long delays' (for so he describes it), Richard Baxter saw his way clear to marrying Margaret Charlton. On 10 September 1662, they began their life together: a union which was to be so beautiful an example of Christian marriage.

For the next nineteen years Margaret's love and companionship cheered and eased Baxter's path. Gone were the fears and depressive moods of her earlier days as she gave herself unreservedly to her God-given task. Her sadness and melancholy vanished, comments Baxter, 'counsel did something to it, and contentment something; and being taken up with our household affairs did somewhat.'

For the first ten years of their life together Richard and Margaret were constantly on the move: harried, persecuted and driven to and fro by circumstance. Sometimes their accommodation was poor, damp and cold. Margaret's health often suffered in consequence. 'In the first year', records Baxter, 'few poor people were put to the hardness she was put to. We could have no house but part of a poor farmer's, where the chimneys so extremely smoked, as greatly annoyed her health.' But in her cheerful acceptance of her lot she displayed a selflessness and courage, which in the words of John Howe, 'gave proof of the real greatness of her spirit.' 'I know not', continued her husband as he looked back on their years together, 'that she ever came to any place where she did not extraordinarily win the love of the inhabitants.'

Margaret revealed unusual spiritual insight and wisdom so that Baxter would often consult her over vexed issues. 'She was better at resolving a case of conscience than all the divines that ever I knew in all my life', was Baxter's estimate of his wife's abilities.

In 1672 came the King's Declaration of Indulgence. Restrictions were eased temporarily and during the following few years Margaret used her resources to rent accommodation where people could gather to hear Baxter preach. Her initiative and ceaseless endeavour were often rewarded by short periods when he could minister unmolested, but always his relentless enemies caught up with him and he would be silenced again, fined or even imprisoned.

But Margaret had never been strong and the physical demands of her new way of life took a heavy toll. It would seem she was a life-long sufferer from migraine head-aches. 'A great pain of head held her from her youth, two or three days every fortnight', Baxter informs us in his *Breviate*, or short account of Margaret's life. The illness of 1659 that had brought her so near to death had also left its scars and she was highly susceptible to lung infections. At last in 1681, and at only fifty-five years of age, she succumbed once more to disease. She seemed to sense that this was her last illness and some of her old fears returned. But although often in pain, Margaret accepted God's purpose for her. 'Lord, I submit; God chooseth best for me' was her testimony of faith. After some days of delirium her mind cleared and she died calling upon her God to help her and show her his mercy.

Ten years of life were left to Richard Baxter and hard years they were, of pain, imprisonment and malicious slander. He missed Margaret sorely, but her memory was a balm to his spirit until he joined her once more on 8 December 1691, as he too entered 'the saints' everlasting rest'.

JOHN OXTOBY
Praying Johnny

Although he was not book-learned, it was knee-work, knee-work, knee-work with him.

HARVEY LEIGH

1. John Bradford.

2. The Birthplace of Richard Cameron at Falkland.

3. Wang Ming-Dao.

4. Susannah Spurgeon, with their twin sons.

5. Margaret Baxter.

6. The Grave of John Oxtoby at Warter.

7. William Bramwell.

8. The Death of Captain Allen Gardiner.

9. Adolph Saphir.

10. Janet, at the age of ten.

8

A middle-aged man stood knocking at a cottage door in a straggling Yorkshire village. Short and thick-set, he had a kindly weather-beaten face, genial smile and light brown hair combed down straight to his eyebrows. His style of dress suggested he might be a farm worker: the old brown coat and equally worn waistcoat, the chocolate-coloured neck-tie and drab cloth gaiters all indicated a certain indifference to personal appearance. At that moment the cottage door swung open and John Oxtoby stepped inside.

The scene was in the village of Warter, not far from York, in 1810, and there was hardly a home in the village where 'Praying Johnny' was not welcomed. But it had not always been so. When he was first converted the situation was far different. His earnest enthusiasm to gain the souls of his fellow villagers for the kingdom of God met with little favour: some thought he was mad; others were angry at his interference in their lives; most were indifferent to his appeals.

John Oxtoby was born in 1767 on a farm at Little Givendale, near Pocklington, about twelve miles from York – a beautiful and secluded spot, but too insignificant to feature even on a detailed map. As a child of farm workers, he received only rudimentary schooling and was cast into life with few prospects. A farm-hand himself, he carefully saved his meagre wages, hoping one day to improve his position, but by some misplaced confidence he was cheated of all his resources. Irreligious and self-indulgent, John Oxtoby was to pass the next twenty-five years of his life with barely a thought for his Creator. His abandoned life and demeanour gave little indication of what he might become by the grace of God.

1804 marked the profound change. The words of an itinerant Wesleyan preacher awakened his conscience to the anger of an offended God and the awesome possibilities of a hell to come. A settled grief rested on his spirit: he could neither eat nor sleep. Day after day, night after night, he cried out to God for mercy until his former companions judged him beside himself. Nor did the Lord grant an immediate answer of peace to Oxtoby's distressed condition: rather it was a struggle protracted over many months. When at last he gained assurance of God's forgiveness through Christ, it was to him a 'pearl of great price'. Now thirty-seven years of age, his desire to bring his family and friends into these same spiritual joys knew no bounds. Though dismayed by the indifference or hostility displayed towards his efforts, John Oxtoby was not intimidated. Gradually, very gradually, his endeavours began to be rewarded with a measure of success.

The village of Warter was typical of many another York-shire village in the early years of the nineteenth century. Little gospel light had penetrated its darkness and men and women lived out their days largely in ignorance of the grace of God. The dramatic change in Oxtoby's way of life was, however, a factor the local people could not ignore. No single cottage or homestead, humble or grand, escaped a visit from this indefatigable evangelist. While at first many a door was slammed in his face, the situation slowly changed.

Once invited inside, John would display sincere concern for the family he was visiting – their troubles, sicknesses and anxieties – and always he would pray with them. So he gained the name, 'Praying Johnny'. And God answered the prayers of this simple and earnest soul-winner. Over the months the whole aspect of the village altered: now there were many families where the gospel of Jesus Christ was believed and loved; now every door opened gladly as 'Praying Johnny' passed by. If for any reason he missed out a home, the aggrieved householder would call out, 'What have we done that we must not have you pray with our family?' Leigh Harvey, writer of a biographical sketch of John Oxtoby, comments, 'Open profanity durst not show itself . . . and many began to pray who before desired not the knowledge of God.' Soon the people of Warter were anxious to have a chapel of their own, and it was Oxtoby who provided both a suitable piece of land and a gift towards the erection of the building out of his slender means.

For the next fifteen years 'Praying Johnny' spent all his strength in promoting the spiritual good of his fellow men through his exhortations and prayers. Conscious of his own wasted years, he travelled ceaselessly through the east Yorkshire villages engaging in personal evangelism among the people. He worked in association with the Wesleyan Methodists but still retained his daily employment as a farm labourer until the end of this period; then he devoted himself exclusively to the work, undertaking his own financial support. As an unmarried man his material needs were few and his way of life simple.

The first decade of the nineteenth century saw the emergence of the Primitive Methodist Connexion. It was a movement born out of revival: born not initially out of great preaching but by a transforming work of the Spirit of God on two or three Staffordshire men. Hugh Bourne, William Clowes and Daniel Shubotham had no intention of starting any new denomination; rather they were men of passionate spiritual energy, men surprised by the work of God in their own souls and quite unable to keep silent about it. Methodism had lost some of its early fire at that time and before long Hugh Bourne and his friends were disciplined and expelled from their local Methodist Society for their insistence on using methods of evangelism disapproved of by the Society.

In 1812 these men, and the numerous groups of believers gathered together as a result of their preaching, formed themselves into a new association. They adopted the name of Primitive Methodism as an expression of their desire to recapture the urgency, passion and evangelistic zeal that had characterised the Wesley brothers, Whitefield, William Grimshaw and other early Methodists. Very few of its founder members were highly educated in earthly terms, but in the school of prayer and faith they were well taught by the Spirit of God. And it was to the Primitive Methodists that John Oxtoby, now fifty-two years of age, joined himself in 1819.

William Clowes, described as Primitive Methodism's 'mighty evangelist', was in Hull at the time. Hull, the scene of his ungodly exploits in his unregenerate days, was now the scene of his most glorious exploits for the kingdom of God. During his first four months in the city four hundred people had been drawn to the Son of God – not attracted from other religious groups, but converted from the world. John Oxtoby, who had been labouring in the villages around Hull, found in Clowes a kindred spirit. Like Clowes he too had a past of unrighteousness of which he was ashamed, and with him he shared that flame of zeal to win the people for Jesus Christ.

John Oxtoby never regarded himself as a preacher. His lack of educational advantage, coupled with little ability at constructing his thoughts into an orderly sequence, caused him to be reticent about any form of public address. He was pre-eminently an example of that gift of Christ to his church which the Apostle Paul describes as 'an exhorter'. He took delight in travelling with William Clowes and after Clowes had preached would assist him by 'labouring with mourners'. It was through this work of personal exhortation that God had transformed the village of Warter and in it Oxtoby excelled.

But he was not called 'Praying Johnny' without good cause. One who worked closely with him has left on record the fact that it was Johnny's habit to spend much time each day in private prayer. Here lies the secret of his extraordinary effectiveness: the explanation of how with sure hand he could lead wounded and anxious consciences to 'the fountain opened for sin and uncleanness'. In public prayer he was equally effective: 'His petitions were generally powerful and prevalent,' comments his biographer, 'in answer to the earnest breathings of his soul a whole assembly has been moved, as the trees of the wood are moved when shaken by a strong wind.'

With this prayerfulness came another and closely allied gift – the gift of faith. Like Abraham, he was 'fully persuaded that what God had promised he was able also to perform.' Many were the stories circulated concerning the amazing answers to Johnny's prayers. One example concerns a Hull man by the name of Stephenson who was in a state of deep anxiety. A ship he owned had been on a distant voyage, but its return was now long overdue. Not only did this good man fear the loss of his money, his vessel and its crew, but to add to his distress, his own son was on board. Repairing to John Oxtoby, Stephenson confided his trouble to him. Johnny knew of only one course of action – he gave himself to prayer and fasting on behalf of his friend. After some time God granted to his praying servant an inward assurance of faith that all would be well: the vessel, with those on board would return safely. More than this, by the inward eye of faith, Johnny 'saw' the vessel itself. So certain was he that he assured Stephenson that he would recognise the boat on its return though he had never actually seen it with his physical eyes.

Stephenson and his family were astonished, even incredulous. But still the weeks passed by without any news. Never did Oxtoby waver from his conviction though his prediction grew daily more precarious. But at last the vessel returned. In exhilaration Stephenson sent a gig to fetch Oxtoby, asking him if he could point out the missing vessel. Scanning the hundreds of ships bobbing up and down in the harbour, Johnny suddenly exclaimed, 'That's the ship which God showed me while at prayer! I knew she would come home safely and that I would see her.' And he was right.

Such inward assurances of faith were not confined to 'Praying Johnny'. In the early days of Primitive Methodism there were many godly men and women who knew the experience of spending long periods in earnest and urgent intercession. If they then received a particular, inward assurance from the God of heaven that their cry was heard – but not without such an assurance – then they would 'rise in faith' from their knees with never a doubt that the petition would be granted.

Even though John Oxtoby had little natural gift for public ministry, he ventured to preach from time to time as he accompanied William Clowes. His intense ardour, his clear perception of the mind of God, his deep love for the souls of men, lent to his words a winsomeness and spiritual grace which compensated for his limited ability. The people clamoured for more. After a year in Hull, John Oxtoby's name began to appear on the local preachers' plan for the Hull circuit. During the next three years he engaged in this occasional preaching until in 1823 William Clowes recognised in his assistant so high a degree of spiritual usefulness that he encouraged him to preach on a regular basis. So it was that John Oxtoby, now aged fifty-six, became an itinerant preacher among the Primitive Methodists and continued in this capacity until his death six years later.

No effort for the kingdom of Jesus Christ appeared too arduous for this determined soul-winner. Harvey Leigh describes his zeal in these words: 'His whole soul panted within him for the extension of the kingdom of God, and the deliverance of immortal souls from the thraldom of sin. He looked on the moral waste before him with the tenderest sympathy to the souls of men, and cast himself into the midst of the work as one who was determined to conquer.' And God owned such earnest zeal. Oxtoby's journal provides us with a record of his labours, breathtaking in its range and result. His main responsibility was for Westgate, in Weardale, then part of the extensive Hull circuit. But though he appeared to be preaching in many different places in the area, sometimes as far west as Carlisle, on each Sunday and often midweek he was back in Westgate.

This journal gives clear evidence of the grace and power of God which accompanied his preaching, yielding its harvest of men and women converted and bringing glory to God:

October 8 [1724]: Preached at Westgate; a pentecostal power came down while we were singing, 'Refining fire go through my heart'. Some cried out, 'O Lord, enlarge my heart!' Many were astonished. Some ran out of the chapel . . . Some were praying with mourners, others rejoicing with believers, and others were singing.

October 26: Preached at Kilhope, and the Lord laid to his helping hand; four got clean hearts. Two men came to scoff; the Lord laid hold of one, and brought him down: every bone in him shook. The other went away wounded.

Many were the attempts on the part of those who opposed such preaching to stir up trouble, some quite ingenious: 'Preached at Westgate at nine and two and at Stanhope at six – a full chapel; the devil raged, and the people put an ass into the chapel.'

Lines written on John Oxtoby well express the popular esteem in which he was held:

> It was yesterday I went to hear
> The man whom all run after;
> Some join to sing and some to pray
> While others make a laughter.
>
> His preaching gifts they are but small
> Or else he don't improve them;
> His words are exhortations all,
> But zealous souls do love them.
>
> When mourning souls are in distress
> He prays from morn till evening;
> Which shows he always feels the best
> When sinners are returning.

Clearly it was not his polished language or reasoned appeal that gained for Oxtoby so willing a hearing: rather it was the constraining grace of God that accompanied his ministry, driving his words to the consciences of his hearers. If there was one place where 'Praying Johnny's' limited abilities might be a disadvantage it would be in the prosperous city of Leicester. When Oxtoby visited a Primitive Methodist chapel there in June 1826 he found fifteen hundred people packed into the building. Hoping to be unobserved, Oxtoby slipped into the building and waited for the preacher to appear. To his consternation he was spotted and asked if he would preach. All unprepared as he was, he had no choice, but God clothed his words with grace and power. Describing the occasion in a letter, Johnny wrote:

I had not preached long before one woman received a full salvation; and she clapped her hands and shouted, 'It is done!' I exclaimed, '*It is done*, only believe!' ... The scene at one time was most extraordinary ... a great number of persons fell to the ground ... some were in deep anguish; some were crying aloud for mercy; and some were made happy in God.

A choice story which lingers on in the history of Primitive Methodism illustrates some of Oxtoby's most admirable characteristics. The Quarterly Meeting of the Association was in progress in Bridlington at a time when the future of the work in Filey hung in the balance. Many efforts had been made to testify to that self-centred and godless town and win a hearing for the gospel there. But all seemed futile: the hearts of the people remained unmoved. Perhaps it was now time to withdraw valuable workers and concentrate on areas that appeared more responsive. John Oxtoby listened to the arguments both for and against such a move, his compassionate heart breaking with sorrow over the prospect of abandoning a town to its unbelief. On being asked for his opinion, he blurted out, 'What do I think? I think the Lord has a great work to do at Filey, and if you will send me I will go and live upon potatoes and salt, and lie on a board if necessary before it shall be given up.' It was decided to send Oxtoby.

Packing his few possessions into a bag, Johnny set off for Filey. 'Where are you going?' asked one of his friends. 'To Filey, where the Lord is gannin to revive his work', came the instant reply. Coming within sight of his destination, Johnny fell on his knees behind a hedge and began to plead with God for the town. A miller chanced to pass that way some hours later and heard some strange sounds emanating from behind the hedge. He thought it was two men arguing, but stopping to listen, he realised it was not two men, but one: it was Praying Johnny. 'Thou munna mak a feal o' me. I told them at Bridlington thou wast gannin to revive thy work, and thou mun dea so or I shall never be able to show my face among them again, and then what will the people say about prayin' and believin'?' Like Jacob wrestling with the angel at Jabbock, so this noble intercessor fought on until assured of an answer of peace. 'It is done, Lord, it is done!' he exclaimed rising from his knees. 'Filey is taken! Filey is taken!' And he was right. As Oxtoby began his work in the town, the people listened with deepening concern and before long the promised revival broke out on all sides, establishing a permanent work of God there. Filey was indeed taken for the Lord of hosts.

Following this floodtide of blessing in Filey, Oxtoby ministered in several northern towns for short periods. In June 1828 we find him in Tadcaster, where 'the wilderness began to blossom as the rose', his biographer informs us. Six months later he travelled to Leeds. Dismayed at first by the filth, both physical and moral, that he found there, Oxtoby was still confident in his God. Writing to a friend he describes the situation: 'It [Leeds] abounds with every kind of wickedness that could be mentioned . . . amidst all this, however, the Lord's arm is not shortened, but he continues to bring sinners to himself.' But John was conscious that his own health was breaking down. He had been asked to move on to Halifax in June 1829 but was hesitant about the appointment. 'The will of God be done', he wrote to a friend. 'If John be sent of God, it will do; if not it will avail nothing.'

Bravely he set off for Halifax at the end of July after another period of illness. But his strength was rapidly failing and by the end of November it became clear that he could continue no longer. Repairing to his sister's home in Londesborough, near York, John hoped to recuperate, but God willed otherwise. The course of his disease seemed to baffle all medical skill and never again did he leave the house until the call came to exchange earth for heaven seven weeks later.

The principles that govern a man in his living will often control him in his dying. And so it was with John Oxtoby. In his life he had held Jesus Christ eminently honourable, and in his death he declared to a friend that Christ was 'present and precious – wonderfully precious to my soul'. To another friend, he added, 'Tell them, all the former manifestations I have had are nothing compared with those I now feel.' In life, a deep concern for the souls of men had been his ruling passion. It had led him into earnest supplication at the throne of grace, and in his death he was still praying. With his powers of speech fast failing, his last whispered prayer was, 'Lord, save souls: do not let them perish.' 'Glory, glory, glory,' were the final words Praying Johnny uttered before he himself was 'received up into glory'.

If you were to visit the village of Warter in Yorkshire – that village transformed by the grace of God through the exhortations of John Oxtoby – and were to climb the steep steps leading into the old churchyard, you would find a well-kept grave near the gate. There on a headstone erected in memory of their village evangelist, and engraved in clearly legible words, are these lines commemorating his zeal and spiritual worth:

> *'Tis not on marble, nor on gilded page*
> *To print thy worth – thy charity display!*
> *For chronicles like these may in an age*
> *Be lost, and in oblivion pass away.*
> *Eternity itself will best unfold*
> *The souls led by thee to the heavenly fold.*

EDWARD PAYSON
This One Thing I Do

The celestial city is full in my view. Its glories beam upon me, its breezes fan me, its odours are wafted to me, its sounds strike upon my ears, and its spirit is breathed into my heart. Nothing separates me from it but the river of death, which now appears but an insignificant rill, that may be crossed at a single step whenever God shall give permission.

EDWARD PAYSON

Fair Beulah land! nor could I think before
Such hidden wonders lay in store
For Christians as they die.
I breathe its fragrant heavenly air,
Celestial music fills my ear,
Pervading all my wakeful dreams,
And even death's dark river seems
To lose its dread, that I
May cross it at a single pace
To greet my Saviour face to face,
Beyond the bright'ning sky.

F.C.

9

'You would greatly oblige me by lending me a copy of your prayer today', said a distinguished visitor as she left Edward Payson's church. Great was her surprise when the preacher replied that the words of his prayer had vanished with the breath that gave them utterance.

Beyond doubt God had anointed Edward Payson with a remarkable gift in public prayer. One who sat regularly under his ministry has described his feelings when he opened his eyes at the conclusion of one of Payson's prayers: '. . . it was always a letting down, a sort of rude fall . . . to find myself still on the earth. His prayers always took my spirit into the immediate presence of Christ, amid the glories of the spiritual world; and to look round again on this familiar and comparatively misty earth was almost painful.' Describing the prayer that Payson offered when visiting his home, another friend wrote:

When he spread forth his hands to God, heaven seemed to come down to earth and the glory of the Lord shone around our tabernacle . . . He knew our miseries and told them all in such tones of tenderness and sympathy, as made us feel that a friend was pleading our cause . . . It seemed as though the cloud of the divine presence covered the household, and the divine majesty was very near us.

This gift of public prayer bore a direct relationship with Payson's own communion with God. He has been compared with David Brainerd (who was also of New

England but lived half a century earlier) for the ardour and passion of his private prayer. Scattered throughout Payson's letters and journal are references to his struggles and conquests in this realm which tell their own story:

May 3. Never before had I such faith and fervency in prayer. I was as happy as nature could sustain and could only say – Blessed Jesus! this is thy work . . .

July 18. Very little comfort in prayer. Have fallen into a sad lifeless state the week past. Hope it will convince me more strongly than ever of my weakness and vileness . . .

Edward Payson was born in Rindge, New Hampshire, in 1783. This was the year of the American Declaration of Independence and a significant year in the divine chronicles for it saw also the birth of Samuel J. Mills, whose passionate concern for the evangelisation of peoples unreached by the gospel led directly to the emergence of American missionary endeavour. Asahel Nettleton, too, was born that year in Connecticut – a man who was to be markedly used in the powerful revivals that characterised the opening decades of the nineteenth century in America.

When these three children were born, spiritual life in New England was in decline. The impetus of the Great Awakening of the first half of the eighteenth century had gradually died away and in the wake of the American War of Independence a materialistic and sceptical generation was growing up. Deism flourished and in many areas vital religion was at a low ebb. But by the end of the century, however, the tide was beginning to turn. Remembering Jonathan Edwards and the Concert of Prayer – harbinger of God's mighty acts – some twenty New England pastors called the people to specific prayer for an intervention from God.

In 1795 Timothy Dwight, grandson of Edwards, became president of Yale College. Profanity and unbelief were widespread in the academic world with Tom Paine and his rationalistic philosophies in vogue while the young people of an independent America were largely strangers to true religion. But Dwight tackled the problem by inviting his students to voice their unbelief freely and then answered it by a series of sermons designed to expose and convict. In 1802 revival broke out and it was estimated that one third of the entire student body of Yale was brought to saving faith.

These were the times in which young Edward Payson grew to maturity. The blood of the Pilgrim Fathers was in his veins and he could trace his family back four generations to an Edward Payson from Essex in England who had sailed in the brig *Hopewell* in 1636, married a fellow passenger, young Mary Eliot (sister of John Eliot who became known as 'the Apostle to the Indians'), and settled in Roxbury. Their youngest son, Samuel, was the father of Phillips Payson who had four sons, all of whom both attended Harvard College and became ministers of the gospel. The youngest of these, Seth Payson, ordained in 1782, was called to become pastor of a church in Rindge, New Hampshire. Here it was that Edward, his eldest son, was born.

A cursory glance through the *Memoir of Edward Payson*, first published shortly after his death in 1827, quickly reveals the profound influence that his mother, Grata, exerted on him. The record is interspersed throughout with their correspondence which continued all his life, for she died only a few months before her son. Grata Payson, who could also trace her lineage back four generations, and to the same family as her husband, was a shining example of Christian motherhood. We are told 'the all-absorbing concern of her soul respecting him was that he might become a child of God.' Although she also had natural desires for Edward's well-being and progress, this one aspiration dominated all else in her thinking. And God abundantly rewarded her prayers and exhortations, for the boy showed evidence of a tender conscience from earliest days. He was known to weep under the preaching of the gospel when only three years of age.

To give an exact date for Edward's conversion would be difficult. His mother, in whom he confided throughout his early years, believed it was in childhood, but his father was not equally convinced. So uncertain was he of Edward's true spiritual state, despite his outwardly unblameable behaviour, that he deferred sending his son to Harvard to complete his education until he was more confident that Edward would not be swept away by the infidelity of other students.

In 1800 Edward began his studies at Harvard. Diligent and quiet, he attracted little attention at first and few were aware of his academic potential. But Edward had a very retentive memory and soon the pace at which the young man could read some massive tome and retain virtually every detail became a cause of general astonishment among his peers. Graduating in 1803, Payson was engaged to take charge of the newly-formed Portland Academy in the northern province of Maine. Portland, destined in God's purposes to be the scene of his subsequent labours as a minister of the gospel, was a delightful coastal town combining the fascination of a busy seaport with the natural beauties of the majestic White Mountains that rose up behind the town.

Edward was now twenty and the contract at the Portland Academy, which was to run for three years, covered a formative and important era in his spiritual development. Coming from a closely knit family, he was deeply affected by the sudden death of a younger brother in 1804. It startled and searched him out. Why had God allowed so grievous a providence to come upon his family? It must be as a chastisement, he decided, and as no other member merited such correction as far as he could judge, he concluded, 'It remains that I am the Achan who has drawn down this punishment and occasioned this distress ... My careless and obdurate heart rendered it necessary, to punish and humble it.'

This sorrow marked a turning point in Edward's spiritual experience. Now he was plunged into a period of intense conviction of sin, of longings after holiness and grief over failure which continued for almost a year. At last he realised that despite his mental appreciation of the biblical doctrine of justification by faith alone, he had still been trying to discover within himself sufficient merit to approach his God. 'I find I have been trying to establish a righteousness of my own', he admitted sadly. Payson's twenty-second birthday was clearly a significant date, marking a renunciation of the enticement and pleasures of this world. A coded entry in his diary, deciphered only with difficulty, reveals that on this day the young man made a solemn covenant with God, ending with the words, 'The vows of God are on me.'

Now there was no turning back. The subsequent course of Edward Payson's spiritual progress was like the arrow that flies with undeviating accuracy to its mark. All his endeavours from this moment were directed to this one end: to serve and please God. Now his private diary and letters became packed with the record of that intensity and passion in secret prayer which held the key to the exceptional usefulness of his short life.

In 1806 Edward relinquished his charge of the Portland Academy and returned to his parents' home at Rindge. Now he was convinced that God was calling him into the ministry and he wished to devote himself to preparation for such an undertaking. Above all he was determined to gain a total mastery of the Scriptures which he studied – verse by verse, line by line – until there was virtually no biblical subject upon which he had not formed an opinion.

At this point Payson inaugurated a rigorous discipline for himself: 'Resolved to devote in future twelve hours to study; two to devotion; two to relaxation; two to meals and family devotions; and six to sleep.' Dissatisfied still, he subtracted two further hours from his sleep and increased his periods of fasting, until like Whitefield before him, he inflicted permanent injury on his health. Alarmed for his safety, his mother and sister would often stand outside his door with a little refreshment, but pleaded in vain for admission. Although Payson retained a weekly fast until the end of his life and strongly recommended the practice to his church members, he freely admitted his own excesses and the subsequent damage caused to his health.

Payson, like many other effective preachers, was a man of extremes of feeling. At times his spiritual joys carried him to the heights until his mind could scarcely sustain the degree of bliss he experienced. But within a few days, sometimes even within an hour, he could be cast into the depths of self-recrimination and despair. One example, recorded on 15 August 1806, must suffice:

Rose in a sweet, tranquil, thankful frame . . . had faith and freedom in prayer. Yesterday I thought God himself could hardly carry me through. But today – O how changed!

In these sharp altercations of mood Payson again resembles David Brainerd.

Payson came from a family noted for its tendency to depression. His biographer comments sensitively, 'He had a constitutional predisposition to melancholy which other branches of his family are said to have shared to a still more painful degree.' In maturer years Payson learnt to discount some of these wide swings of mood and his varying 'frames', understanding better that his feelings were not a satisfactory guide to his true state. In addition Edward suffered from indifferent health all his life. Severe migraine headaches left him prostrate with pain and sickness for many days at a time; and in later years insomnia compounded all other problems. A double fall from his horse in 1807 dislocated his arm, leaving a permanent injury that caused him frequent discomfort and led finally to a paralysis of the damaged arm.

In August 1807 Edward Payson was back in Portland, this time to preach at the Congregational Church whose pastor was looking for an assistant. Possibly he planned to spend only a short time there, but was to remain for the rest of his life. So great was the enthusiastic reception for his ministry that Payson accepted a call from the church and was ordained on 16 December of that year. 'Rose very early', he records, 'and renewed my covenant with God, taking him for my portion and giving myself up to him for the work of the gospel ministry.' But Payson was an ill man at the time. Symptoms of tuberculosis had become apparent immediately before his ordination and developed so rapidly afterwards that he thought himself to be dying. He struggled on for some time but soon was obliged to return to Rindge to recuperate until the summer of 1808.

When he had recovered sufficiently to resume his ministry, Payson's preaching immediately caused a stir in Portland. In devastating terms he exposed the wickedness of the human heart: its pride, malice, cruelty and devilish treachery. Such words evoked a strong reaction, setting the town in an uproar. In mock seriousness one unbeliever would now greet another in the street as, 'Brother devil'. But Payson's denunciations were not spoken harshly; rather they sprang from a heart that yearned over his fellow men and felt their impending judgment acutely. Even harder to bear was the reaction of his own church members, some of whom were offended at such preaching. 'My people are raving about my hard doctrine', he comments sadly. Added to this pressure, Edward faced financial insecurity, for the Embargo Act, placed by Congress on American farm products in an attempt to put pressure on France and Britain, was self-defeating and brought industry in Portland into severe recession. It looked as if Payson would not be able to continue there for long. Such a situation might well have daunted many young preachers, but Edward persevered and by the following August could tell of over forty enquirers and many others under serious concern of soul.

By the end of his first year in Portland, despite his periods of ill-health, twenty-nine new members had been added to the church. And yet the burden on Payson's heart remained for the many who appeared to reject the message he preached: 'O, my friends, my dear friends,' he pleaded in a sermon marking his first anniversary as their pastor, 'how do our spirits droop, and our hearts sicken with anguish and despair when we consider that notwithstanding all we can do, many here present will find the gospel "a savour of death unto death", and all our exertions will answer no other purpose than to increase beyond conception their misery and guilt! O, ye precious and immortal souls . . . hear and obey ere it is too late! Tell us, O tell us how we may draw or drive or lead you to Christ!'

For the next twenty years Edward Payson ministered in Portland and eventful years they were. God was favouring his people with revival in many parts of the land and Payson's soul burned to see demonstrations of God's power among his own congregation. During 1809 a further forty-two had shown serious concern for salvation and the same number again in 1810, with another thirty in 1811. Such divine favours would surely have filled most preachers with astonishment and delight. But Payson could not rest satisfied. Each year he prayed, longed and prepared for revival blessings and each year recorded his despondency that no exceptional work of God had taken place. Payson searched his heart, fearing lest he himself should be the obstacle to the outpourings of God's Spirit. Indeed, he attributed the premature breakdown in his health in part to his repeated and heightened expectations followed only by a crushing sense of disappointment as the hopeful indications died away. And yet the yearly average of likely conversions throughout his entire ministry was at least thirty-five and the year of his death saw seventy-nine new members added to the church.

In December, 1811, the senior minister relinquished his position, leaving the entire care of the congregation to Edward Payson, who was now twenty-eight years of age. His days were packed with activity: 'I preach, or do what is at least as laborious, six nights a week, besides talking incessantly a considerable part of every day', Payson wrote in a letter, for there were many awakened to their spiritual need and seeking counsel at that time. Yet it was in this same year that he found time to court and marry Louisa Shipman!

Edward had once expressed the fear that he could never marry because his tendency to emotional extremes might mean that he would so over-love a wife and family that he would evoke God's displeasure. But in Louisa he found a partner of excellent worth: stable, wise and well-equipped to counter-balance her husband's volatile nature. Simple rules of godliness governed their family life: 'We have agreed that if either of us says a word which tends in the least to discredit another person, the rest shall admonish the offender; and this has entirely banished evil speaking from among us.' If he was at home in the early evening, Edward informed his mother, 'we all sit down and take a little tour up to heaven and see what they are doing there. We try to figure to ourselves how they feel . . . and often . . . our own feelings become more heavenly; and sometimes God is pleased to open to us a door into heaven, so we get a glimpse of what is transacting there . . . and we can scarcely wait till death comes to carry us home.' In this practice we can trace the influence of Richard Baxter, one of his favourite authors.

Eight children were born to Edward and Louisa, four boys and four girls, though two of the girls died in infancy. Edward, who had a natural genius for inventing stories, was a devoted father to his children. They brought a tenderness and balance into the rigour of his self-discipline, enriching his family life with many moments of light-hearted fun. One of his daughters, Elizabeth Payson Prentiss, who was nine when her father died, has described his presence as 'my happiest spot on earth'.

Although Payson continually grieved that no widespread revival occurred in Portland, the year 1816 stands out as one of significant spiritual favours. 'My whole soul was gradually wrought up to the highest pitch of eager expectation and desire,' Edward confessed; 'my mind is on a rack of suspense and I can scarcely support the conflict of mingled anxieties, desires and expectation.' In the event he could report about seventy seekers and meetings so crowded that believers were often obliged to stay at home to leave room for those wishing to hear the preaching. A new building had to be erected, holding five hundred worshippers, and Payson could write, 'Christ is so precious and my cup runneth over.'

Despite the fact that Payson grieved because the scale

of divine favour resting on his labours was not as widespread as he might desire and for which he so earnestly prayed, yet his name was to become a fragrant memory throughout New England for many decades following his death in 1827. (Elizabeth Prentiss mentions that babies called after her father could be numbered in hundreds, if not thousands, during that period. On a single day in 1852 she noted that the newspapers recorded the deaths of at least three little 'Edward Paysons').

Payson's printed sermons, which were eventually to run into six volumes, began to appear shortly after his death, but not even these accounted for the widespread and lingering influence of his ministry. His preaching had a charm all its own which held his hearers spellbound by an ardour and urgency that few could resist. There was 'an unaffected earnestness, a glowing intensity of feeling . . . a manner wholly original and indescribable', writes the editor of a selection of his sermons published in 1831. The stark alternatives of the gospel were so impressed on Payson's own mind that they found expression in every sermon and always he addressed others with a deep awareness of his own sin: 'I never was fit to speak a word to a sinner except when I had a broken heart myself . . . and felt as if I had just received pardon to my own soul – no anger, no anger', he was to write at the end of his life.

Above all it was Payson's devotion to Christ and to a life of prayer that infused his entire ministry with grace and power. Among the highlights of the worship at Second Church in Portland (for there were three Congregational churches in the town) was the communion service. These occasions were a delight to Payson's own soul – a foretaste of the heavenly feast. It was as if he shared with his people his own spiritual exercises. It seems appropriate, therefore, that one of his last commitments in July 1827, just three months before he died, should be to preside at a communion service.

Edward was only forty-four, but his health was so broken that his congregation knew his time among them was short. The paralysis of his arm had now extended to other parts of the body, his voice was so weak that a false ceiling was installed in the church to reduce the strain, and those headaches which had caused lifelong distress now became prolonged and violent. One present at this communion service has left a description which can best be told in his own words. Speaking of Payson, he writes:

His body was so emaciated with long and acute suffering that it was scarcely able to sustain the effort once more imposed upon it, but his soul, filled with a joyful tranquillity, seemed entirely regardless of its mortal tenement . . . I have never known Dr Payson so abstracted from earth than on this occasion . . . In all the glowing fervour of devotion, he contemplated the Saviour as visibly present in the midst . . . There was a breathless silence and I can say, for one, that the terrors of hypocrisy never swelled so fearful, and the realities of the judgment seat never seemed nearer than at that solemn hour.

On 5 August Edward Payson made his last public appearance. Too weak now to take much part, he watched – overcome with emotion – as twenty-one people were received into membership. Many crowded round him afterwards wishing to shake their beloved pastor's hand for the last time.

Edward Payson died triumphantly. Long years of meditation on 'the rest that remains for the people of God' had prepared him to overcome the relentless assaults of the 'last enemy'. Only a month before he died he was to say:

Last night I had a full clear view of death as the king of terrors; how he comes and crowds poor sinners to the very verge of the precipice of destruction, and then pushes them down headlong! But I had nothing to do with this . . . I felt that death was disarmed of all its terrors; all he could do was to touch me and let my soul loose to go to my Saviour.

Throughout the following weeks friends, church members and his family remained around him and for each he had unforgettable and challenging words.

Now robbed of almost all power of movement and often in acute pain, Edward was still utterly happy. Speaking to a young convert, he said:

Christians might avoid much trouble and inconvenience, if they would only believe what they profess: that God is able to make them happy without anything else . . . To mention my own case – God has been depriving me of one blessing after another; but as every one was removed, he has come in and filled up the place; and now, when I am a cripple, and not able to move, I am happier than I was in all my life before, or ever expect to be.

He still exhorted his church members as they came to visit him in small groups. To some of the young people he said:

And now standing as I do on the ridge that separates the two worlds, feeling what intense happiness or misery the soul is capable of sustaining . . . my heart yearns over you, that you may choose life and not death.

As the month of September wore on, Payson's physical distress grew worse, but his spiritual joys more intense. 'If my happiness continues to increase I cannot support it much longer', he confessed. His views of the heavenly city became brighter every day, until he could exclaim: 'When I read Bunyan's description of the Land of Beulah, where the sun shines and the birds sing day and night, I used to doubt whether there was such a place; but now my own experience has convinced me of it, and it infinitely transcends all my previous conceptions.' On 19 September he dictated a letter to his sister – a letter which must surely hold a unique place in the recorded experiences of dying Christians:

Dear Sister,

Were I to adopt the figurative language of Bunyan, I might date this letter 'from the Land of Beulah' of which I have been for some weeks a happy inhabitant. The celestial city is full in my view. Its glories beam upon me, its breezes fan me . . . and its spirit is breathed into my heart. Nothing separates me from it but the river of death, which now appears but an insignificant rill, that may be crossed at a single step, whenever God shall give permission. The Sun of Righteousness has been gradually drawing nearer and nearer, appearing larger and brighter as he approached, and now he fills the whole hemisphere; pouring forth a flood of glory . . . A single heart, a single tongue seems altogether inadequate to my wants . . .

And now, my DEAR sister, farewell. Hold on your Christian course but a few days longer, and you will meet in heaven,

Your happy and affectionate brother,

EDWARD PAYSON

A few more weeks of suffering were left for this valiant servant of Jesus Christ and on 21 October 1827 he spoke his final messages of love to the family he was leaving, his youngest son being only a year old at the time: 'Peace! peace! Victory! victory!' he exclaimed, and looking at Louisa he added tenderly: 'I am going, but God will surely be with you.' The last words he could articulate were 'Faith and patience holds out!' So passed from this earth one of the church's noblest sons: a man of prayer, a man of God.

CATHERINE BOSTON
'Gainst Storm and
Wind and Tide

A woman of great worth, whom I therefore passion-ately loved, and inwardly honoured: a stately, beautiful, and comely personage, truly pious, and fearing the Lord . . . patient in our common tribulations, and under her personal distresses.

THOMAS BOSTON
A tribute to his wife

10

When the twenty-one-year-old Thomas Boston first met Catherine Brown it was clearly a case of 'love at first sight'. In his own inimitable style, Boston tells us in his *Memoirs* that when he saw her 'something stuck with me'. A few days later they met again. This time he records his attraction to her 'piety, parts [gifts], beauty, cheerful disposition'.

In the following year, 1698, the two became engaged but another two years were to pass before circumstances were right for them to marry. In spite of an undeniable preaching gift, Thomas Boston had found continual problems in settling with a church. Several different congregations would have wished to call him, but his way was constantly blocked by the 'heritors' or landowners who had the final say in any appointment. This system of patronage had been a perpetual source of trouble in the Scottish church and remained so for many years to come.

At last in 1699 the small parish of Simprin and its heritor were of one mind in a decision to invite Thomas Boston to become its minister. Situated eight miles south-east of Duns and ten miles west of Berwick-on-Tweed, Simprin would not have been Boston's natural choice. It was a small rural community numbering fewer than one hundred adults. Nor could the parish provide Boston with suitable accommodation: the old manse was in ruins and for the first three years of his ministry Boston lived in rented accommodation while a new manse was being built. But by diligent waiting on God, Boston overcame his natural aversion to the place and was able to record, 'My soul is well satisfied with the determination.'

On 17 July 1700 Catherine Brown and Thomas Boston were married. The ceremony, conducted in a private house as the custom was, and with only a few relatives and friends present, took place between eight and nine o'clock in the evening. Thomas was now twenty-five years of age and Catherine twenty-seven. Little could they guess how many sorrows and trials lay before them in their lives together; but thirty years later and just two years before his death, Thomas recorded one of the most beautiful and tender tributes that any man could ever have paid to his wife. He describes her as:

a woman of great worth, whom I therefore passionately loved, and inwardly honoured: a stately, beautiful, and comely personage, truly pious, and fearing the Lord; of an evenly temper, patient in our common tribulations, and under her personal distresses: a woman of bright natural parts, an uncommon stock of prudence; of a quick and lively apprehension, great presence of mind . . . sagacious and acute in discerning the qualities of persons . . . modest and grave . . . but naturally cheerful; wise and affable in conversation . . . and finally, a crown to me in my public station and appearances . . .

Well could Thomas Boston say with the writer of the Book of Proverbs, 'Whoever finds a wife, finds a good thing and obtains favour from the Lord.'

Catherine joined Thomas in the temporary accommodation allotted to them until the manse was ready. Already he had established regular morning and evening worship with his household and gave himself with unremitting diligence to the preparation and delivery of sermons for his people. Seldom in good health and suffering frequent periods of depression as a result, Thomas found in Catherine a partner who could console and stimulate him. Thomas Boston remains one of the outstanding figures in Scottish church history but the debt he owed to Catherine cannot be underestimated.

In May 1701 Catherine's first child was due. She herself was the daughter of a medical man and probably for this reason knew more than most about the perils of childbirth. Boston records that Catherine had a 'great terror of the pains of child bearing', and not without cause, for he continues, 'she had an uncommon share of these pains, the remembrance whereof to this day makes my heart to shrink.' Before her confinement she 'laid her account with death', in this way preparing herself to face the last enemy if God should so ordain. On 24 May a little girl was safely born and also called Catherine. But the joy of the birth was marred, for the new-born child was disfigured by a double harelip. When Thomas, hurrying to see his wife, was given this news his 'heart was struck like a bird shot and falling from a tree'. He adds, 'my afflicted wife carried the trial very christianly and wisely after her manner.'

As in every other painful circumstance of his life, Thomas Boston searched his heart to try and understand any lessons God might be teaching him through the trial. And there were compensations too, for as he and Catherine watched over the frail little girl, he records, 'In that dear child's case, I had a singular experience of tender love melted down in pity.' After about six months little Catherine began to thrive and so Boston thought it would be safe to leave her with a nurse while he and his wife attended to some business at Catherine's family home. During their absence Catherine had a vivid dream. In her dream she saw her baby perfectly restored from her disfigurement and strangely beautiful. So striking was this dream that Thomas and Catherine hurried home as soon as possible. They were greeted with the sad news that the baby had died. Her death had taken place, as nearly as they could judge, at the very hour that the dream was given.

In April of the following year, 1702, a son was born, a fine-looking little fellow, whom they called John. Boston remarks, 'in his appearance our hearts were comforted after the heavy trial of his sister.' Within a year another son, Robert, was also born, but this child lived only twenty-one months. His death coincided with a period of considerable difficulty in the work at Simprin. Thomas Boston was seeking to raise standards of discipline in the parish and for this was 'reproached through the country'. It was a double trial but Boston comments that Catherine was 'helped to carry the burden very christianly'.

In 1705 a second daughter, Jane, was added to the family, a child who was to become a particular comfort to Catherine and Thomas and in whose birth Boston recognised a signal providence in view of the trials that lay ahead. Throughout these years Catherine was frequently unwell, suffering many debilitating headaches. Each of her confinements took a heavy toll on her health both physically and nervously, and in addition Thomas himself was far from robust. Yet during this period in Simprin he ministered faithfully to his 'handful', as he sometimes called his parishioners. The sermons he preached, carefully written out in manuscript form, became the basis of his first and best-known book – *Human Nature in its Fourfold State* – a work widely owned of God and still in print today.

During 1706 Boston was increasingly exercised about the possibility of a call to Ettrick, a scattered rural parish south-west of Selkirk, in the Scottish Border country. As usual he waited long and earnestly on God that he might be sure that his motives for desiring such a move were

God-honouring. Catherine was expecting another child and early in 1707, as Thomas was meditating and praying over the possibility of a new sphere of service, he had particular freedom to pray for Catherine and the unborn child. If it should be a boy, he would call him Ebenezer, meaning 'Hitherto hath the Lord helped us'. It would be an expression of gratitude to God for his past goodness and a token to assure themselves of his present guidance and care.

On 23 April 1707 little Ebenezer was born, just a week before Boston was due to take up his ministry at Ettrick. Thomas and Catherine rejoiced together and took this birth to be a significant expression of God's favour and blessing on their home and on the ministry that lay ahead. When baby Ebenezer died four months later, it was a grief hard to be borne. 'To bury his name', Boston confessed, 'was harder than to bury his body.' He found it difficult to understand this providence in the light of the particular significance attached to his birth. And if Thomas found the grief so acute, it is not hard to imagine how Catherine must have felt.

Again there was no suitable accommodation for Thomas and Catherine and the two children, John and Jane, in Ettrick. While a new manse was being built, they lived in the stables and barn belonging to the old demolished manse, which had been roughly partitioned to make extra rooms. Here in the barn, in August 1708, Catherine's next child was born. The confinement was difficult and Catherine was very ill afterwards. The newly-born little boy lay for some days without a name while his father struggled over the issue, well remembering his last experience. Eventually he determined that if Catherine should recover, he would re-enact his faith and call his infant son Ebenezer once more. It was to him a covenant with God but this time he would hold its human symbol with a less tenacious grip.

When the other two children contracted measles, little Ebenezer also became ill and died at just seven weeks old. But God upheld the grieving parents and Boston records: 'In the day of distress the solemn covenant was sweet and my heart was thankful to the Lord . . . While he was drawing his last breaths, he so smiled, that the sight of it made my heart to leap.'

During the next twelve years Thomas Boston was actively involved in the public affairs of his church, often playing a lonely and courageous role in upholding truth. The parish of Ettrick, at first so resistant to Boston's ministry, was transformed by his preaching and throughout this period he laboured with diligence and prayer to prepare the *Fourfold State* for the press. Catherine faithfully supported him, running the household as efficiently as her chequered health would allow. Two more children joined the family circle, Alison in 1711, and Thomas in 1713. Two others died, including a last baby daughter in 1716, once more called Catherine. This final bereavement caused much grief, 'That child was very comfortable to me', records Thomas sorrowfully, but adds, 'I bless him I was helped to part with her and saw and believed much of the Lord's goodness in that dispensation.'

We may well imagine the effect of all these trials on Catherine. Of the ten children she had borne, only four survived and her many difficult confinements further undermined her precarious health. In January 1720 Jane, who was fifteen, became seriously ill with smallpox and for some time her life hung in the balance. Perhaps this period of anxiety contributed to the onset of a more serious malady that overclouded all the remaining years of Catherine's life. May 10, 1720 was a day Thomas Boston and his family could never forget. 'It was a day remarkable above many to me and my family,' Thomas explains, 'being that wherein my wife was seized with that heavy trouble, which hath kept her all along since that time unto this day, in extreme distress.'

It would appear that from this period onwards Catherine suffered from an acute form of mental disorder, which distorted some aspects of reality, leaving her a prey of distressing inward and inexplicable fears. The condition, complicated by her continued poor health, made Catherine an easy target for Satan's onslaughts, both concerning her assurance of salvation and her peace with God. But God supported her and Boston writes: 'Nevertheless, in that complication of trials, the Lord hath been pleased . . . to make His grace in her shine forth more bright than before.'

At first the illness was intermittent, proving worse in the summer months, but gradually it became more dominant and by 1725 Catherine was virtually housebound. But there were still periods of remission. Whenever the dark clouds rolled back, all Catherine's lovely personality sparkled out again with its accustomed brightness and in spite of the effects of illness and ageing she retained something of her former attractiveness. More importantly, in these short periods of relief her faith shone out as clearly as ever. Of one such occasion Boston records: 'She thought within herself . . . that when the promise comes not in, the sinner may go out unto it, and seek it . . . accordingly she set herself to gather promises, and got them abundantly.'

By 1726, however, Catherine's condition was worse, and now she seldom left her bed. Thomas describes her pitiful state in these words: '. . . free among the dead, like the slain that lie in the grave, remembered no more; being overwhelmed with bodily maladies, her spirits drunk up with terror.' But in spite of it all, in many areas her conversation and thought remained as lucid as ever and God supported her with additional measures of his grace. 'The Lord has at times given her remarkable visits in her prison and manifested his love to her soul.'

Earnest supplication was raised to God on Catherine's behalf and Thomas was often sorely perplexed when no clear deliverance was granted. 'Now were we, with our broken ship within sight of the shore, . . . but behold, in a little time after, the storm rose anew; and the ship was beat back into the main ocean again.' But the grace of God continually upheld Catherine and brought her soul into a firmer assurance of faith than she had ever known before. In 1728, eight years after her illness began, she described one such experience.

On 21st March betwixt two and four o'clock in the morning, on my bed of affliction . . . I did with the whole bent of my soul, embrace the everlasting covenant held forth to me in the word of the gospel of grace; I did cast myself over on the Lord Jesus Christ and did receive him in all his offices; I did take God to be my God in him and with my whole heart gave up myself, soul and body, to be the Lord's for ever. . .

In August of that same year Catherine recorded a covenant made with God, clearly based on that remarkable night in March:

August – I do this day solemnly covenant and give up myself to be the Lord's, and I accept Christ upon his own terms, and in all his offices, and I do firmly expect the outmaking of the precious promises, which I believe are more firm than the mountains of brass with respect to all the difficulties in my lot in the world and my throughbearing in death . . . As witness my hand. Catherine Brown.

From 1724 Thomas Boston's own health had been steadily deteriorating. His days were filled with study as he prepared his sermons, checked through his numerous manuscripts for publication, and attended to the pastoral needs of his scattered parishioners. He also toiled unremittingly at gaining an understanding of the accentuation of the Hebrew Scriptures, believing that thereby he might uncover some further revelation from God's word. Often in pain and weakness himself, he was always burdened with Catherine's sad condition.

In 1732 at the age of fifty-six, Thomas Boston died, a few years before Catherine. During the final months of his life he had been preparing a small book for the press: *The Crook in the Lot* (the title was derived from Ecclesiastes 7:13 and refers to any one predominant trial in a person's life). Published posthumously, it dealt with the sovereignty of God in relationship to the afflictions of his people. The material, first given as sermons, was etched out of the sufferings that Thomas and Catherine had endured together. Thomas had sometimes found it hard to comprehend why God should have appointed such a troubled path for them both. The answer must surely lie, at least in part, in this little book, for through it God has taught countless other Christian people to accept with meekness those sufferings appointed for them by a sovereign and merciful God:

The crook in the lot gives rise to many acts of faith, hope, love, self-denial, resignation and other graces; to many heavenly breathings which otherwise would not be brought forth.

William Bramwell
Man of Prayer and Power

The records of Methodism are crowded with examples of saintly living: but from among them all, no instance of profounder piety can be cited than that of William Bramwell.

ABEL STEVENS

His powerful preaching and fervent prayers were so mighty through faith that the stoutest-hearted sinners trembled before him.

THOMAS PEARSON OF GOMERSAL

11

A little-known itinerant Methodist preacher arrived at his new appointment in the West Riding of Yorkshire in 1791. William Bramwell found religion in Dewsbury in a sorry state. Friction between believers had nearly destroyed the cause of Christ among the people. Dismayed by all he saw, young Bramwell gave himself to earnest prayer. This had proved effectual in the past and he knew of no other solution. 'A year of hard labour and grief' ensued, but Bramwell prayed on. Then God gave him a secret indication that his prayers had been heard. Bramwell has left on record these remarkable words:

As I was praying in my room, I received an answer from God in a particular way, and had the revival discovered to me in its manner and effects. I had no more doubt. All my grief was gone; I could say, 'The Lord will come: I know he will come, and that suddenly'.

We are told that in the following three months at least one hundred people were converted and joined the Dewsbury Methodist Society, and many believers were quickened 'to greater diligence and activity in the work of the Lord'.

Who was William Bramwell? Why should William Booth, of Salvation Army fame, name his eldest son *William Bramwell* Booth? In his *History of Methodism*, first published in 1856, Abel Stevens provides an answer. 'For more than thirty years he was one of the most successful preachers of English Methodism', he comments, adding,

'It is doubtful whether any other Methodist preacher of his day was directly instrumental in the conversion of more souls.'

Born in 1759, in the village of Elswick, ten miles from Preston, Lancashire, William was the tenth child of George and Elizabeth Bramwell's family of eleven. As conscientious members of the established church, George and Elizabeth taught their children to be scrupulous in their attendance to religious duties. The Scriptures were highly regarded and the Lord's Day was observed with meticulous care. Truthfulness was continually inculcated and integrity of character encouraged. Such an upbringing laid a noble foundation for young William's life, though as yet no ray of gospel light illumined his soul.

At the age of sixteen, William was sent to Liverpool to join his older brother in business. But the boy could not settle, and the wickedness he observed all around troubled his sensitive conscience. Appreciating his son's difficulty, George Bramwell recalled William and soon apprenticed him to a tanner in Preston. Here he worked well and gained the respect and confidence of his master.

William was a serious boy and throughout these years the Spirit of God was at work convincing him of sin and urging him onwards with an almost insatiable thirst for the knowledge of God. Late at night he would read the Scriptures by candlelight; and when his master prohibited this, fearing that loss of sleep might affect his work, William crept downstairs long after everyone else was in bed and tried to read by the light of the dying embers of the fire that still glowed in the grate.

Tortured by an increasing sense of the inward sinfulness of his heart in God's sight, William turned, like many before him, to ascetic practices to try and ease his burdened conscience. He knew no better way. Sometimes he would cut his fingers deliberately, at other times sprinkle coarse sand on the floor and kneel for many hours through the night begging forgiveness for his sins. He allowed himself little relaxation. While the other apprentices enjoyed a free day, William would steal away to the woods, climb a tall tree and spend the day crying out to God for mercy. Though six feet tall and strongly built, William's health began to suffer under such privations. But God had heard his cry and came swiftly to his aid. As he partook of the bread and wine at the Lord's Supper, he suddenly knew his sins pardoned. His biographer, James Sigston, comments:

Darkness and gloom, guilt and condemnation, were at once removed in a manner incomprehensible to him, and utterly beyond all that he had been taught to expect or desire. The height of his joy was equalled only by the depth of his previous sorrow.

From this moment William Bramwell gave himself in unremitting endeavour to the promotion of those truths that had brought light and liberty to his own soul. No effort was too great, no expenditure of energy too costly. He reproved profane language at every opportunity, even offering his friends money if they would desist from their customary oaths. But as yet he knew none of like mind with whom he could share his experiences; nor had he ever heard evangelical preaching of the grace of God.

In Preston there was a small group of Methodists and one young man from among them, Roger Crane, hearing of Bramwell's zeal, tried to befriend him. But William's prejudice against 'the sect' was profound. Taught by his parents to suspect and despise all Methodists, he firmly resisted any invitation to attend their meetings. But God had his own means of sweeping aside William's biased views. A local woman, a notorious blasphemer, had been giving vent to her accustomed execrations in his presence, so William wrote her a note, warning her of the fearful destiny awaiting her unless she repent, and pushed it under her door. Her reaction was to call Bramwell 'a Methodist devil'. When this was reported back to William he commented, 'My Bible tells me, "They that will live godly in Christ Jesus shall suffer persecution", and these people are much vilified and persecuted.' He decided at that moment that he must find out more about the Methodists.

Soon William agreed to listen to Methodist preaching and recognised instantly the truths concerning the grace of God in Jesus Christ that had been made real to his own soul by God's Spirit and declared, 'O! this is the kind of preaching I have long wanted to hear. These are the people with whom I am resolved to live and die!' His parents, chagrined and angry at their son's decision to join the Methodists, threatened to cut him off from all further financial help, but William was undeterred by such intimidation, though continually solicitous of their spiritual welfare.

While the assurance of pardon for his sin brought peace of conscience to Bramwell, it did not lessen the intensity of his desires after holiness of life. An inner dissatisfaction on account of daily failure and sin often robbed him of spiritual joy. Shortly after his conversion, William had the privilege of meeting the aged John Wesley for the first time. Perhaps the wise old man sensed young Bramwell's inner conflict, for he looked at him intently and then asked, 'Well, brother, can you praise God?' 'No Sir', replied William honestly. 'Well perhaps you will tonight', came the rejoinder. And so it was, for that very night William received further assurances from God of his love and forgiveness. Still Bramwell yearned for more. He had heard the Methodists talk about 'receiving entire sanctification' and 'being cleansed from all known sin'. If such blessings were available to the believer, William desired with all the ardour of his passionate heart to possess them.

It must be said at once that teaching which claims such perfection to be possible in this life is a doctrinal aberration and in conflict with clear biblical principles. But if these believers were in error over the *interpretation* of their spiritual experience, the divine blessings which came to them in seeking earnestly after holiness and perfection, certainly in William Bramwell's case, bear all the hallmarks of authenticity. With undeviating purpose he set himself to seek this mercy from God:

I was for some time deeply convinced of my need of purity, and sought it carefully with tears and entreaties and sacrifice; thinking nothing too much to give up, nothing too much to do or suffer, if I might but attain this pearl of great price.

God heard his petition and visited him when he was least expecting it, shedding abroad his love in the young man's heart. In Bramwell's own words: '. . . heaven came down to earth; it came to my soul. The Lord for whom I had waited came suddenly to the temple of my heart . . . My soul was then all wonder, love and praise.'

With such zeal, coupled with new joy in God, William soon found opportunities for serving Christ by preaching among the rural people in the villages near Preston. God owned his ministry in a remarkable manner and many who were converted and edified through it urged him to offer his services to the Methodist Connexion as an itinerant preacher. William hesitated. His high view of the ministry coupled with a profound sense of personal unworthiness threw him into an agony of indecision. Often he hid himself away on the moors or in the woods, earnestly begging for divine guidance.

Eventually his prevarications were ended by a providential intervention. Repeated letters from Dr Coke, one of Wesley's principal assistants, urged Bramwell to fill a vacancy in the Canterbury circuit. William Bramwell decided to go. He must leave a newly-established tannery business, his recently-purchased home, his ageing parents and above all the girl who had just agreed to marry him. But counting all loss for Christ's sake, he bought a horse, packed his saddle bags and rode off into the winter of 1785 – a hazardous three hundred miles – to far-off Kent. He was now twenty-six years of age.

Bramwell found the Methodist societies in Kent in a parlous condition with dissension and division on every side. It was enough to fill even the most seasoned preacher with dismay. Though the evident blessing of God rested on his labours in the Canterbury circuit, the work was arduous and often Bramwell struggled against depression or was tempted to relinquish the task and return home. But in these very circumstances he was to learn valuable lessons which were to play a vital part in his future ministry. His first step was to establish gatherings for prayer in private homes, often at five o'clock in the morning before the people dispersed for the labour of the day. These times of united prayer proved unforgettable:

Frequently when at prayer, so powerfully did he wrestle with God that the room seemed filled with the divine glory, in a manner the most extraordinary; which made some persons ready to imagine the very boards shook under them.

But such power in prayer had not been easily attained. William Bramwell had long made his personal communion with God of primary concern each day and in many of the letters addressed to fellow ministers he urges the vital necessity of private prayer. Writing to John Hanwell, itinerant preacher in the Bridlington circuit, he exhorts, 'Rise early. Never be in bed late, unless you are obliged to sit up late. Pray! Read! Pray!' This advice clearly suggests Bramwell's own priorities, for not only did he give himself to a life of spiritual devotion, he also believed in the importance of an informed and biblically competent ministry. Stevens, the Methodist historian, tells us that Bramwell devoted much time to a study of the Scriptures. He was fully conversant with French, translating a book on preaching from that language into English, and also acquired a working knowledge of Hebrew and New Testament Greek.

Under the Methodist system established by John Wesley, the preachers seldom remained more than two years in any one circuit and in 1787 Bramwell once again headed north and joyfully claimed his patient bride, Ellen Byrom, whom he had not seen for more than eighteen months. For the next thirty years, until his sudden death in 1818, he preached mainly in the north of England, staying only two or three years in most areas. Leeds, Sheffield, Sunderland, Newcastle and Hull were among the places where his ministry was remarkably blessed. As in America, so also in England, these were years when God was pleased to demonstrate his power in repeated revivals in far-flung parts of the land. Between the years 1792 and 1840 accessions of believers to the non-conformist churches could be numbered at about one and a half million people, or one out of every ten of the population. In the Wesleyan Methodist churches alone membership (which excludes those who were adherents only) had risen from 72,000 in 1792 to 245,000 in 1828, and this despite the various divisions and secessions these churches had experienced.

Social conditions during these years were grim with widespread deprivation and misery. The Industrial Revolution had resulted in a vast migration of the people from the countryside to the towns, bringing disruption to whole communities. Squalid little terraced dwellings, hastily built, back to back, housed large numbers of people in the fast-growing towns. Hours of employment were excessive, with child labour rife. Added to this the French Revolution cast a shadow of fear across a community also seething with social discontent. The Napoleonic wars that followed made life and trade insecure with repercussions of famine and hardship felt mainly by the working people. The price of corn had tripled between 1792 and 1812.

Against this background the searching and rousing preaching of William Bramwell challenged and edified the people, and many there were who learnt to lift their eyes from the depressing scenes of daily life and set their hearts on eternal treasure. The big man with eyes 'piercing as an eagle's' was endowed by God with many natural pulpit gifts. 'Few', reports Stevens, 'had such control over public assemblies, repressing excesses, awing opposers ... His voice was singularly musical, his command over the passions of his hearers absolute.' Preaching was to Bramwell a momentous and solemn undertaking. He would tolerate no disturbance from his congregation. No crying children were allowed to disturb the worship, nor would he permit any other distraction. Every eye had to be fixed on him at all times. If he observed any loss of concentration he would stop and wait, judging it an insult to God rather than man. But it was the spiritual power pervading all his preaching, praying and personal conversation that distinguished his ministry even in those remarkable days.

Mere statistics can give little insight into the profound impression that Bramwell's preaching had upon the people. The man himself was his sermon. His own personal integrity and spiritual standards were well known and every fibre of his being was concentrated into those penetrating and demanding messages. Salvation from the degradation of sin with its eternal consequences and the imperatives of godliness on all who professed faith were his twin themes. But such preaching was costly; to a friend Bramwell admitted, 'The Lord knows, I die a death every time I preach; I do not know how I have lived so long.' And confiding in a fellow minister, he refers to the price and rewards of such preaching:

I frequently tremble exceedingly before I go into the pulpit. Yea, I wonder how I ever dared engage in such work. Yet when I am labouring to speak a little, I am frequently so much over-powered by the divine presence, that I would not leave my work for all the world . . . Go on, my dear brother, preach, pray, purge, and plant.

After his period at Dewsbury, William Bramwell was appointed to the Birstall circuit, near Leeds, in 1793. Here similar displays of the converting power of God accompanied the preaching, as Bramwell and the people gave themselves to urgent intercession. Over five hundred were reported to have been added to the Society during Bramwell's time there. 'No man can ever fast and pray in vain', he afterwards maintained, for here in the Birstall circuit he had proved it true.

Anticipation ran high in the Sheffield circuit when news of Bramwell's appointment there in 1795 became known. Accounts of the manifest grace of God in Dewsbury and Birstall heightened expectations among the people. Nor were they disappointed. But this was no superficial excitement; we are told:

The humble, the broken-hearted, the thirsty for God, were encouraged NOW to believe in Christ . . . Under his awakening appeals untold numbers have trembled; the veil of ignorance and the mask of hypocrisy were torn away.

An eye-witness account confirms the nature of the extraordinary work of God which followed:

Certainly if ever I knew or experienced pentecostal seasons, it was at this time, when if not thousands, at least hundreds were added to the Church; many of them, I doubt not, such as shall be eternally saved. The arrows of conviction fastened on many; conscience did its office; 'Gallios' became serious; before the presence of Jehovah the stout-hearted bowed the stubborn knee, and rocks of impenitence flowed into streams of penitential sorrow . . . It seemed that there was but a thin veil between us and the invisible world, and that Satan for a season was bound in chains . . . Many were pressing through the strait gate into the kingdom which is 'righteousness, peace, and joy in the Holy Spirit.' . . . How often was the large floor of the Norfolk Street chapel to be seen clustered over with little groups around a wrestling Jacob! and when he 'halted a little on his thigh', how ready were many to administer a word of consolation, how ready to join in prayer that shook the pillars of hell and opened the gates of heaven.

James Sigston, Bramwell's principal biographer, estimates that twelve hundred were added to the Methodist churches during his first year in Sheffield, with a further five or six hundred the following year. Such was the floodtide of blessing which accompanied Bramwell's preaching.

From Sheffield Bramwell was sent to Nottingham. Here again his ministry was owned by God with an abundant demonstration of his mercies. 'Such glorious displays of the Lord's omnipotent power and of his willingness to save perishing sinners, I believe will never be forgotten by hundreds who then partook of the divine blessing', wrote one who was there. And this remained the pattern wherever Bramwell went, though with decreasing intensity as the years passed on. He returned north once more in 1801, back to the Leeds vicinity; and in 1804 conducted a memorable ministry in Hull, on the east coast. In 1806 he travelled further north to Sunderland, then across to Liverpool and back again to Sheffield in 1810.

William Bramwell was now fifty-one, and from this time his health began to deteriorate as he experienced periods of serious illness. His years had been packed with activity and intense physical exertion. Never content until he saw God manifest his power in revival, he regularly rose at four o'clock in the summer and five o'clock in the winter to devote time to prayer. He ate sparsely and frequently covered between thirty and forty miles on foot each week, preaching in the outlying areas of his circuit. When appointed to London in 1814, William was hesitant. As a Northerner he was ill at ease over the prospect of ministering to 'the rich and the great'. But relying on the help of God and begging the prayers of his friends, he agreed to go. But he sorely missed the bracing air of home and after some months both he and his wife became ill. William was afflicted with severe rheumatic pains and it was judged unwise for them to remain in the south for another winter. So in 1815 Bramwell was appointed to Newcastle. Throughout his letters in these years we find constant reference to the approach of death and the glory beyond. For some time he appears to have had a secret intimation from God that he would die suddenly. This he had already confided to close friends, but now he felt it would be soon. Writing to his daughter Ann in 1815, he confesses:

When I first came to Newcastle I had, as I thought, reason to believe that I should be taken home from this place. The impression was such as made me speak of it to a few friends. In this I look up, and must say, 'thy will be done!' May I be ready every moment.

In the same letter he also tells Ann of a remarkable visitation of God to his soul, perhaps given to prepare him for the glory to come:

I hope you will unite in praise to God when I tell you that I have received what I call an extraordinary baptism of the Spirit . . . My soul has experienced such a fellowship with God and heavenly things, as I never felt before. O the glory which shall be revealed! I am swallowed up in him!

The Salford circuit, near Manchester, was to be Bramwell's last appointment; here he went in 1817. An even greater urgency now seemed to characterise his preaching. 'Bear with me, O bear with me,' he would exclaim, as he returned again and yet again to the issues of life and death, sin and salvation. And all the time he longed for Christ's appearing, which he regarded as imminent. As he expressed it in a letter to a friend, 'I am always waiting to leave this body, that we may be clothed upon with our house in heaven. Glorious company! Glorious place! I long, I wait for his coming!'

The annual Methodist Conference held in Leeds in 1818 was to be Bramwell's last. He knew the end was near. In a prayer offered during that week his hearers afterwards recalled him praying, 'Lord, didst thou not speak to me today and say, "Thou shalt soon be with me to behold my glory?"' Leaving the Conference a few hours early, he went to the home of his friend, James Sigston, where he was to spend the night before catching an early coach back to Manchester.

But it was not the coach for Manchester that came for William Bramwell that night: rather it was the chariots and horsemen of heaven. Retiring to bed late after hearing last reports from the Conference, he hoped to snatch a few hours' sleep before his journey. In the event he spent the time in prayer instead. One staying in the same house in an adjacent room caught fragments of his words: 'O Lord, prepare me for thy kingdom, and take me to thyself', he pleaded. At half past two in the morning Bramwell returned downstairs, ate a little breakfast prepared for him by Alice, the servant girl, prayed with her and then set off into the night.

Moments later running steps could be heard outside. Alice opened an upstairs window and peered out anxiously. 'There's a man dying in the lane', called a voice. Waking the family in alarm, Alice unlocked the door and they all hurried out to see if they could render any assistance. But they were too late: William Bramwell 'was not, for the Lord had taken him'.

ALLEN GARDINER
Dying and Behold We Live

I am passing through the furnace, but blessed be my heavenly Shepherd, He is with me, and I shall not want. He has kept me in perfect peace and my soul rests and waits only upon Him. All I pray is that I may patiently await His good pleasure, whether it be for life or for death; that whether I live or die, it may be for His glory.

ALLEN GARDINER
From his last letter to his wife,
written a week before his death

12

Allen Gardiner was a born adventurer. Even during his childhood one master-ambition governed his thought and play: to explore unknown lands and sail the high seas. Born in 1794 at Basildon, in Berkshire, Allen Gardiner was the child of Christian parents, and in later years expressed his gratitude to God for such a privilege. Understanding their fifth son's dedication to a life of travel, Samuel Gardiner and his wife allowed Allen to enter the Royal Navy cadet college in Portsmouth, in 1808, when he was fourteen years of age.

After two years of training Allen had his first long-anticipated experience of a sea voyage, and for the next twelve years served on many different ships, becoming acquainted with some of the remotest regions of the earth. Throughout these years Gardiner showed no apparent interest in spiritual truths but nor could he quite shake off the influence of the early training he had received. The surreptitious purchase of a Bible on one visit to Portsmouth betrayed a hidden anxiety over his neglect of his father's God. Two events at this time were used by God to bring about a profound change in Gardiner's life. The first was the death of his mother. He received this news when his vessel was docked off the coast of China. It was a sharp and painful reminder of former days and of one whose faith and prayers he could never forget.

While these thoughts were fresh in his mind, Allen Gardiner happened to visit a Buddhist temple in inland

China. Here he witnessed the futile and misguided devotion of false religion. The contrast between this and his parents' faith was real and startling and led directly to Gardiner's own conversion to God. The profound change in his thinking is reflected in his journal; and in August 1822 he wrote:

Adoring my God for his goodness in not having consigned my soul long ago to the terrors of his indignation, I would carefully examine my heart as to the sincerity of its professions and humbly implore at the throne of grace, pardon for all that is past and assistance to guide and strengthen me for the time to come.

In 1823 Allen Gardiner returned to Britain and in July of that year married Julia Reade. But after a few months together he set sail once more and in 1826 was promoted to become captain of his vessel. Family responsibilities, however, coupled with concern over Julia's own health, at last determined Captain Gardiner to relinquish his sea-faring life, temporarily at least. Of the five children born to Allen and Julia, three died in infancy, but the severest blow fell when Julia herself finally succumbed to a condition that had been steadily worsening for some years, and died in 1833. Grief-stricken though he was, Gardiner's faith shines out from the pages of his journal:

My earthly comforts have been removed, and I pass my days in sorrow. Blessed be God! He remembers that we are dust. In my deep affliction he has not left me without mercy and great sources of comfort. The chief of these is drawn from a review of the manifold grace and love which he vouchsafed to my dear wife, making her last days the brightest and happiest of her life . . . It is only my earthly affections that weep . . . I sorrow not as those who have no hope, but have every encouragement to make my calling and election sure . . .

Following this bereavement Captain Gardiner's mind

turned once more to distant lands, but now the passion of his life was the desire to spread the truths of the gospel amongst the peoples he had encountered on his world-wide travels. It was an era of rapidly expanding missionary endeavour. Gardiner was born just one year after William Carey sailed for India. Doubtless he would have heard of Carey's heroic toils and of the exploits of John Morrison, who dared to pioneer an opening for the gospel in China in 1807. Gardiner was now nearly forty years of age; and since 1794, the year of his birth, no fewer than thirteen missionary societies had been established in Britain. The Christian public had become alive at last to the plight of vast multitudes of men and women across the face of the globe entirely unreached by the gospel of Jesus Christ.

To the continent of Africa, called 'the Dark Continent', Allen Gardiner's thoughts were now drawn. In particular he longed to reach the Zulu tribe, renowned for its ferocity, and untouched by the Christian message. But the times were unpropitious for such a venture. Dingarn, the notorious and ambitious king of the Zulus and his tribe, had been involved in warlike exchanges with the Dutch settlers, so any white man was now regarded with intense suspicion. His friends begged him to reconsider his decision, but Gardiner was adamant. Only four months after Julia's death he set sail for the Cape.

The story of Allen Gardiner's encounters with that Zulu king, his skilful handling of the intrepid warrior, and his extraordinary escapes from danger, make fascinating reading. Dingarn's gift of territory to the British Crown (land on which the town of Durban was later built), filled Gardiner with high hopes for the success of his mission. Returning to England, he presented the needs and opportunities among the Zulu people to the Church Missionary Society. In December 1836 he journeyed once more to

Africa, this time accompanied by his children and Elizabeth, his new young bride – only half his age. He was also accompanied by a fellow missionary commissioned by the C.M.S. Soon after his return, however, tribal warfare flared up again, and this, coinciding with animosities between Dutch and English settlers, made missionary work impossible. Sadly, Captain Gardiner and his companions were obliged to abandon their endeavour. 'Disappointed but not cast down,' commented Gardiner in his journal, 'willing to be used or laid aside at his own good pleasure.'

Captain Allen Gardiner wasted no time. The ship that bore his party away from the African coast was bound for South America and at Rio de Janeiro they disembarked just one month later, in June 1838. Pressing far inland, Gardiner established a home for his family, and from there set out to reach the aboriginal peoples, trekking across the Andes and into Chile.

Pioneer work seldom yields easy rewards and Gardiner faced continual setbacks and disappointments as he battled against fears, superstition and Satanic hindrances. Wherever he turned, he seemed to encounter insuperable obstacles. Failing to secure an opening for missionary operations in Chile, Gardiner tried to set up a base in Papua New Guinea. This also proved impossible. At last in 1841 his roving imagination fixed on the wild and windswept islands of Tierra del Fuego, south of Patagonia. At least he could establish a temporary centre in the Falkland Islands where the British flag had first been raised in 1766. From there he could reconnoitre the area weighing up the possibilities for missionary advance.

But wherever he turned the pattern was the same. The Indians of Tierra del Fuego seemed as resistant to his endeavours as any of the other tribes people. Constant pilfering of mission property, and hostile behaviour prevented any permanent work being established among them. So in 1843 Gardiner returned to Britain and attempted to raise support for missionary enterprise in South America. He travelled up and down the country, addressing meetings, writing reports, making appeals, but all his efforts met with apparent apathy on the part of existing missionary societies and the churches. Finally, in 1844, Gardiner founded a new society, called the Patagonian Mission, and then set out once more with one assistant.

Throughout the following four years Gardiner continued his tireless efforts to reach the aboriginal tribes of South America. Despite continuing setbacks, he steadily gained experience; slowly he discovered the most effective methods of winning a hearing for the gospel in those areas. At last, by 1848, he had formulated a plan which he felt was most likely to succeed. He would return to Britain and raise enough support to purchase a vessel able to withstand the ferocious winds and treacherous coastline of Tierra del Fuego. He would take with him adequate stores and equipment to last for twelve months and a team of experienced and dedicated workers. The mission would be stationed on board the vessel to keep their property safe from native pilfering. Contact with the tribes people would be made from there; if a threatening situation developed, it would then always be possible to retreat to the safety of the boat. The plan sounded foolproof.

Once again, however, Gardiner found it impossible to raise sufficient funds for the enterprise. Rather than abandon the idea altogether, he then proposed a modified and less expensive plan. Two smaller launches would suffice, each with landing craft. Provisions for six months would be taken and instructions sent to the Falkland

Islands ordering supplementary stores to be sent to the missionary party at six-monthly intervals. If Gardiner felt any misgivings about the scheme, he did not betray it to his mission supporters, and by his sanguine enthusiasm he won their approval.

A mission party was soon assembled: Richard Williams was a surgeon with no experience of a life of hardship, but a man of earnest Christian faith; John Maidment was a young man known for his zeal and piety and Joseph Erwin was a joiner by trade, whose skills would be a valuable asset to the group. Erwin was devoted to Captain Gardiner, remarking that to be with him was like heaven on earth, for he was such a man of prayer; yet he himself had no personal faith when he embarked on the mission. Three Cornish fishermen, hardy men of the sea, completed the party; uneducated they were, but in full sympathy with the aims of the expedition. They had been brought up in the village of Mousehole, had worked together all their lives, and all shared the name of John: John Badock, John Bryant and John Pearce.

On 7 September 1850 the little party set sail from Liverpool on the *Ocean Queen*, with the mission boats, *Pioneer* and *Speedwell*, on board. Elizabeth Gardiner and the family remained in Britain. On 5 December the *Ocean Queen* reached Tierra del Fuego, and the missionary party disembarked on a small island just south of the mainland in a bay called Banner Cove. Two weeks later the ship sailed away, leaving the seven men behind with sufficient provisions to last until June. There seemed to be mountain goats on the island and there was a plentiful supply of wild birds which could provide fresh meat. What no-one knew as the *Ocean Queen* gradually disappeared from view, was that she was carrying away in her hold their precious stock of gunpowder. It had been overlooked: there would be no fresh meat once their small supply of gunpowder was exhausted.

The initial concern was to find a suitable and sheltered harbour where the launches would be safe from the remorseless Atlantic gales. But in the attempt to find such a place, both the dinghies, which were being towed behind the launches, broke loose and sank. The *Speedwell* eventually managed to gain the shelter of a bay on the mainland, called Spaniard Harbour, but the *Pioneer* was dashed against a tree root in a cove over a mile away and was irreparably damaged. Only six weeks had elapsed since the departure of the *Ocean Queen* and the little party was now stranded at Spaniard Harbour in danger from the Indians, with both dinghies and one of the launches lost. They had no alternative but to wait there until some rescue ship should arrive. The broken launch they dragged ashore that it might serve as living accommodation for half the party. The situation was grievous but Captain Gardiner's faith did not waver. 'He knows our distresses,' he wrote in his journal, 'and is abundant in loving kindness and mercy, and in his own good time can and will (if it be good for us) send relief. On him alone I depend.'

By early March rations were running short. Richard Williams, the surgeon, was the first to be taken ill with a condition he quickly recognised as the dreaded sea-scurvy. Unused to a life of hardship, he had little natural resistance to poor diet and rough conditions. Gardiner had hoped that in spite of the lack of fresh meat, a plentiful supply of fish would compensate for the loss. But this was not to be. With all their skill the three Cornish fishermen were unable to bring very much ashore and as the Antarctic winter progressed, heavy blocks of floating ice damaged the nets beyond repair. And still the little party watched and waited for a relief ship to come to their aid.

The immediate priority was now to attempt a return to Banner Cove to collect any provisions that might still be there and to paint a message on the cliff face indicating the whereabouts of the mission party should any vessel come in search of them. It was a hazardous enterprise with one small boat and a sick man on board. In the event few provisions were retrieved, for the natives had discovered where they were hidden, but a notice was inscribed on the rocks: 'Gone to Spaniard Harbour', large enough for any ship to see from a distance.

Back in Britain serious difficulties had arisen over arrangements for a ship to call at Tierra del Fuego. No shipping company was prepared to undertake the insurance risk for so unprofitable an undertaking. A friend of the Patagonian Mission made three separate arrangements for ships to call but through lack of adequate communications these, too, all went unheeded. Elizabeth Gardiner, sensing that all was not well, addressed a letter to the Falklands requesting help. This also was lost.

In Spaniard Harbour once more, the party split up. John Maidment and Captain Gardiner slept in the broken hull of the *Pioneer*, exposed to the hazards of wind and storm. By day they sheltered in a nearby cave which they dubbed Pioneer Cavern. The other five men shared the warmer, but cramped, conditions on the *Speedwell*. By May the Antarctic winter had set in. It was now highly improbable that any ship would be able to risk the savage conditions to bring relief to the party. Each day Gardiner walked the mile and a half across the beach to check on conditions on board the *Speedwell*. He ensured that the sick men (for John Badock was now also confined to his bunk with the same condition as Williams) had the best of the rapidly dwindling rations.

In his wasted condition Richard Williams recorded his spiritual conflicts and fears in his private journal: 'Satan has urged his fierce assaults upon me at the time of my greatest weakness. I had not strength enough to read nor indeed to pray . . . But faith was more than conqueror, through him that loved me and gave himself for me.' He began to hold services from his bunk for the four others. It was at this time of extremity that Joseph Erwin, so long a stranger to inward and personal religion, cried to God for mercy and forgiveness.

The little group on board the *Speedwell* now enjoyed a sweet spiritual unity. Williams was able to record: 'We are able, by the blessing of God, to make our abode a very Bethel to our souls, and God we feel and know is here. John [Badock] often smiles through a tear that flows from a heart full of the sense of God's love.' Badock's death came first: weakened by the sea scurvy, he had little stamina to withstand the lack of food. He had been labouring for breath, but unexpectedly raised himself up saying, 'Shall we sing a hymn?' Then in a clear voice he began:

> *Arise, my soul, arise,*
> *Shake off thy guilty fears:*
> *The bleeding Sacrifice*
> *On my behalf appears.*
> *Before the throne my Surety stands,*
> *My name is written on His hands.*

Then he was gone. Five men gathered on the beach for a short funeral service. By now they recognised the very real possibility that they might all perish there on that lonely shore. Gardiner was to record: 'My suffering companions endure all without a murmur, patiently waiting the Lord's time to deliver them, and ready, should it be his will, to languish and die here.'

Gardiner still walked each day from the *Pioneer* to the *Speedwell*, but it was becoming increasingly difficult, for he was fifty-seven years of age and his own strength was rapidly failing. Rations were now all but exhausted and soon Gardiner could no longer walk across to the *Speedwell*. Then it became as much as he could manage to scramble out of the *Pioneer* to spend the day in the cave. Maidment did all that he could to find food, but often they were reduced to wild celery and some indigestible mussels. On 7 August Gardiner recorded a prayer, the burden of which was for grace to endure and for others to be raised up in their place to bring the gospel to those desolate islands:

I know, O Lord, there is a deep necessity for this trial, or thou wouldst not have sent it . . . may thy Holy Spirit work in me the grace of true contrition, and renew in me the graces of love, faith and obedience.

A week later Gardiner recorded, 'Today I am from necessity obliged to keep my bed, with little expectation of again leaving it, unless it shall please the Lord in his mercy and compassion to relieve us.' Two days after this Joseph Erwin staggered across to the *Pioneer* to see how his beloved Captain Gardiner was faring. It was a final act of devotion for a week later it was John Pearce who came across the beach to say that Erwin was nearing the end. Gardiner records: 'Thus one and another of our little community is gathered by the Good Shepherd to a better inheritance, and to higher and more glorious employments. Our times are in his hands.'

When John Maidment, now also deteriorating, dragged himself across to the *Speedwell* to bury Erwin he found that John Bryant had also died, unexpectedly and alone. Single-handed he had to bury his two companions, for John Pearce, only twenty-one years of age, was too distraught with grief to help, and Williams was now delirious. The effort was more than his weakened frame could stand. Gardiner recorded in his journal: 'Maidment was so exhausted yesterday that he did not rise from his bed till noon, and I have not seen him since, consequently I tasted nothing yesterday.'

Realising that he also was dying, John Maidment had decided to take himself into the cave to spare Gardiner the effort of caring for him.

It was now 2 September. Gardiner managed to crawl from his bunk to scoop up a little fresh water that trickled from a small stream under the boat. There was little else to do; he wrote a last letter to Elizabeth, one to his son and another to his daughter. On Friday, 5 September, he recorded a final entry in his journal: 'Great and marvellous are the loving kindnesses of my gracious God. He has preserved me hitherto, and for four days, although without bodily food, without any feelings of hunger or thirst.'

His strength was nearly spent. But his thoughts wandered to the other boat. Were Pearce and Williams still alive? He would write to Richard Williams, telling him his fears concerning Maidment. Slowly and with difficulty he wrote, dating his letter 6 September 1851, 'The Lord has seen fit to call home another of our little company. Our dear departed brother left the boat on Tuesday afternoon, and has not returned since. Doubtless he is in the presence of his Redeemer whom he served so faithfully.' His strength was ebbing fast; he could scarcely write any more and the words grew faint and can hardly be deciphered: ' . . . Yet a little while . . . the Almighty to sing the praises . . . throne. I neither hunger nor thirst, though . . . days without water . . . Marvellous kindness to me . . . sinner.'

He may have tried once more to leave the boat in search of water. Perhaps this time he was too weak to scramble back . . . And it was beside his boat that Allen

Gardiner's body was found four months later when at last
a rescue ship came in search of the party.

Therefore are they before the throne of God and serve him
day and night in his temple . . . They shall neither hunger
any more nor thirst any more . . . for the Lamb who is in the
midst of the throne will shepherd them and lead them to
living fountains of waters.

But the sacrifice and sufferings were not in vain.
Horrified by the tragedy, Christians were at last aroused
to action. A schooner of adequate size was purchased; it
was named the *Allen Gardiner* and was used for many
years to fulfil Gardiner's long desire: to bring the gospel of
Jesus Christ to the aboriginal peoples of South America.
Words spoken by the Apostle Paul of his sufferings were
to be true also of Allen Gardiner and his dedicated men:
'As dying, and behold we live'.

THE SAPHIR FAMILY
Finding the Messiah

My whole body is ruined. In heaven there will be no pain. I praise the Lamb slain for us . . . I am happy; my body is decaying . . . scorched with the heat of affliction, but within I am strong in my God and rich in him. Heat takes away the dross and prepares a transcendent joy. I do not dread to die; the Conqueror of death has taken away its sting.

PHILIPP SAPHIR

> *O Conqueror of death and hell,*
> *O Lamb for sinners slain,*
> *Come, set my life above the reach*
> *And tyranny of pain.*
> *For ruined stands this earthly house –*
> *My tenement of clay,*
> *As I await my house from heaven*
> *Beyond decay.*
>
> *Strong in my God and rich in him*
> *No more I dread to die,*
> *For pain is but God's instrument*
> *To sift and purify.*
> *Then let affliction's scorching heat*
> *All taint of dross destroy;*
> *Prepare my soul to comprehend*
> *Transcendent joy!*

F.C.

13

As his camel plodded rhythmically through the heat of the Sinai Desert, Dr Keith grew more and more sleepy. Overcome at last, he slid helplessly from the camel's back and landed heavily in the hot sand. Quickly the camel train was brought to a halt, but anxiety turned to humour as Dr Keith, who appeared unhurt, was helped to remount and progress was resumed. A trivial incident it may well seem, but its repercussions were to be incalculable in the purposes of God.

The year was 1838 and Dr Keith, together with Robert M'Cheyne, Andrew Bonar and Dr Black, was taking part in a deputation from the Church of Scotland to discover areas of potential opportunity for evangelisation among the Jews both in Europe and the Middle East. The party was on the final stage of their outward journey, travelling by camel across the vast tract of desert between Egypt and Palestine. The consequences of Dr Keith's fall proved more serious than was at first supposed, so he and Dr Black cut short their exploration of Palestine in order to return to Scotland. Contrary to their original plans, they decided to travel up the River Danube, resting briefly at Pesth (now Budapest), where they intended to stay only a few days.

Here they discovered to their amazement an unexpected opportunity for the spread of the gospel among the Jewish population. Once again an unforeseen providence interrupted their plans, detaining the two men in Pesth far beyond their original intention. Both men fell seriously ill:

they had contracted a virulent infection known as the Danube Fever. Its onset, in the case of Dr Keith, was sudden and dramatic. He collapsed in the street and had to be carried back to his hotel where he remained in a coma for over six weeks. His condition appeared hopeless; and Dr Black, lying in an adjacent room, was unable to do anything to relieve his friend.

But help was at hand, and from a most unlikely source. The Archduchess, in her magnificent palace overlooking the blue waters of the Danube, heard of the plight of the two Scotsmen, one of whom was apparently dying. This woman had been prepared by God for this moment. Secretly taught by his Spirit to cast herself on Christ for mercy and forgiveness, she had been praying daily for opportunity to promote the spiritual good of the people of Pesth. First the Archduchess brought timely aid to the two sick men, then warmly and insistently invited them to return to the city and work amongst the people, promising all possible assistance.

On their return to Scotland, Dr Keith and Dr Black wasted no opportunity to press both the need and opening for a mission to the Jews in Pesth. At first there was little enthusiasm for such a venture, but Dr Keith incessantly urged that missionaries should be appointed. At last he gained his desire and the following year, 1841, the Church of Scotland set apart four men for this undertaking. Among them was Dr John Duncan, familiarly known as 'Rabbi' Duncan, whose thorough knowledge of Hebrew equipped him admirably for the task.

The missionaries received a warm welcome from the Archduchess, who quietly did all she could to facilitate the endeavour. Under normal circumstances no missionary work in Hungary, a staunch Roman Catholic state, would have been possible. But the presence of some English workmen in Pesth provided an excuse for beginning services of worship, ostensibly to meet their needs. Gradually a few Jews began to attend these services – and old Israel Saphir was among them.

Highly respected among the Jewish community, Israel Saphir was motivated at first by a desire to improve his English. But as he spoke week by week with the missionaries, his interest deepened. Gradually John Duncan's arguments, as he ably demonstrated the harmony between the Hebrew Scriptures and the Christian New Testament, began to penetrate Saphir's defences. A Hebrew scholar, merchant and educationalist, the old man had much to lose. Forty years' study of Judaism had brought him universal respect as the most learned Jew in Hungary – the Gamaliel of their community. Coupled with this, his close friendship with the chief Rabbi gave him added status. So he faced a protracted inward struggle: 'It is hard', he confessed, 'to give up in old age opinions cherished from youth and never doubted.' Yet spiritual light was dawning and Saphir would seek out the missionaries during the week, plying them with searching questions. Dr Duncan's own intimate knowledge both of the Hebrew language and its literature gradually confounded his objections.

Never did Israel Saphir come alone. Always he was accompanied by his young son, Adolph, to whom he was deeply attached – and a strange contrast they presented: the father, now turned sixty-three years of age, leading a fair-haired boy of eleven. Together they listened with grave attention, the young boy fastening his intelligent blue eyes steadily on the preacher's face. A frail and timid child, little Adolph showed early signs of unusual academic ability. By the age of nine he had passed through all the classes at his school, exhausting the resources of the school curriculum to instruct him further. As he was too young for entrance to senior schools, his education was continued through private tuition. More importantly, the child had a tender and loving nature with a marked sensitivity of conscience towards evil.

Bound together so closely, it is appropriate that both father and son should have come to faith in Jesus as true Messiah and Saviour of his people almost simultaneously. One of the missionaries has recorded an account of a communion service in 1842 attended by Israel Saphir and his boy as observers: 'I can never forget *that* sight', he writes, 'Old Saphir was sitting on a chair; the boy was standing between his knees, his young head reaching nearly to the aged face, the face nearly resting on the youthful head. We had ended the Supper. Dr Duncan gave out the sixty-fourth paraphrase, 'To him that loved the souls of men.' To our surprise the voice of the old Hebrew rose above our voices, and when we looked to him the tears were falling plentifully on the head of Adolph. These are days to be remembered.'

But it was little Adolph who first declared his newly-found trust in the Christ, long promised, long awaited. At the meal table the child begged that he might give thanks; this he did, but unexpectedly concluded his prayer by offering it in the name of Jesus. This signalled the way for Israel Saphir to make known his faith also, regardless of the price he might have to pay. Denunciations followed swiftly. The chief Rabbi, so recently his close friend, preached against him in public. Next came intimation that he was shortly to be expelled from the synagogue unless he resigned of his own accord. This he did and also relinquished his position as principal director of the school he had supervised for so long. A bitter cup it was for one of Israel Saphir's standing, but now, fully convinced of the truth, it was one he dared not refuse.

The effect of Saphir's conversion on the Jews of Pesth was dramatic. Some mocked, some reviled him, many wept and begged him to reconsider. But one thing was certain: they could not lightly dismiss such an astonishing change. In every Jewish household the issues these things raised were hotly debated. That a man held in such universal esteem should now publicly own to a lifetime of mistaken opinion shook the community to its foundations. Saphir's reputation for integrity and wisdom prohibited any from suggesting his conversion was counterfeit. Many began to examine the Christian Scriptures avidly and the missionaries soon found themselves scarcely able to handle all the enquiries. Within eighteen months of Dr John Duncan's arrival in Pesth, thirty-five baptisms had taken place.

Israel Saphir was anxious to delay his own baptism until he could bring his entire family with him. Excluding an older son of a previous marriage, this consisted of his wife, Henrietta, two sons and three daughters. From the outset Adolph seemed to be marked out by God in an exceptional manner. 'I feel confident that this child, if he is not being prepared for a speedy removal to another world, is being prepared for much good in this', commented one of the missionaries. The boy took delight in secret prayer, spending much time alone in this exercise, often with tears streaming down his face. Particularly he prayed for the conversion of his mother to whom he was devoted.

A gentle and attractive woman, Henrietta Saphir often appeared careworn. The burden of family life took a heavy toll on her strength and fear of the opinions of others often left her anxious and troubled. Her husband Israel's interest in Christianity, followed by his conversion, presented her with a perplexing dilemma. If she were to follow him, she too might be ostracised and suffer the loss of friendship and social standing. But Israel and her much-loved little son Adolph were praying. Before long Henrietta also began asking the same earnest questions and at last declared herself convinced that Jesus was indeed Saviour and Messiah. The change was radical. John Duncan writes, 'On her countenance there sparkled a joy which I had never seen there before. In fact formerly she always looked miserable. Her talents . . . have also received a wonderful expression through the force of truth.' Soon two of Adolph's older sisters, who were living at home, also became concerned to receive instruction from the missionaries and would often join their young brother in his times of prayer.

Philipp, Israel and Henrietta's nineteen-year-old son, differed from the other members of the family in his spiritual pilgrimage. He had been a wild and careless youth, throwing off the restraints of his orthodox Jewish home to seek worldly gratification. One who knew him described him as 'a loveable yet foolish and disgraceful lad.' A natural catastrophe in Pesth which led to severe flooding and considerable loss of life sobered the young man and he determined to reform his ways and live in accordance with strict Jewish laws. But he remained dissatisfied. In 1842 Philipp came into contact with a German missionary, Charles Schwartz, who was passing through Pesth. Philipp was deeply impressed by his preaching, but it was while he was involved in caring night and day for another missionary who had suffered a serious accident that his quest for truth and reality finally ended. His frequent contact with this Christian man provided many opportunities for spiritual conversation until Philipp Saphir too was converted.

Only Elizabeth Saphir remained unaffected. Devout by nature, thirteen-year-old Elizabeth strove to fulfil every rite and custom in the rabbinical law. During this critical period in the Saphir home, Elizabeth was absent, staying with an uncle who was an orthodox Jew. The bond between Elizabeth and her uncle was deep and he had asked her father if he might adopt her. Israel Saphir would not consent to this proposal but allowed his daughter to prolong her visit. Shortly after his conversion he summoned her home, anxious that Elizabeth too might share the blessing so recently come to the family. Happy to be home, she was at first oblivious of all that had happened. After a few days Elizabeth began to notice the astonishing changes around her and started to make enquiries. But when her father explained that they had found that Jesus of Nazareth was none other than the promised Messiah and Saviour of his people, Elizabeth was stunned. Her own family had become apostates: her grief was overwhelming. She herself would most certainly have nothing to do with such ideas! Wisely, Israel Saphir did not press Elizabeth and urged his family to exercise restraint. Instead he begged her to read the New Testament carefully, searching out the truth for herself. But all the family were praying and their joy was full when Elizabeth declared herself convinced that the New Testament Scriptures were indeed the Word of God. Like Adolph, Elizabeth had a shy and retiring nature and loved to spend long hours alone with the Scriptures. Soon she expressed her wish to be baptized with the rest of her family.

June 7, 1843 was a date never to be forgotten in the Saphir family. Rising early that morning, the children sang and prayed together. The service itself was tense and hushed, the room packed with Jew and Gentile alike, gathered together to witness the baptism. Old Israel Saphir stood in the midst of his family and spoke on their behalf. He told of the inner struggle between grace and sin, experienced by everyone converted to God and of the added conflict between Judaism and Christ which they had faced. All listened with a death-like stillness; many wept as this Jewish family openly identified itself with the redeemed of Jesus out of every nation. The city of Pesth was shaken with the news and for many days this baptism was the sole topic of conversation in public places. If no more were known of the Saphir family than what has already been told, it would still be a significant enough record of the triumphs of the grace of God over tradition and nationalism. But there is more to tell; each member lived out the rest of his or her life, whether long or short, to the glory of Jesus Christ and the good of his church.

Philipp's brief lifespan is a remarkable testimony on its own. Shortly after his baptism he left Pesth to train as a teacher in Carlsruhe Seminary and threw all his energies into his work, often studying sixteen hours a day. Predictably he undermined his health and soon had to relinquish his training. His future was now in doubt. 'Shall I be able to complete my studies?' he asks in a letter. 'Ah! my joy in the prospect of being a teacher was perhaps too great.' He was able to return to the seminary briefly but soon became ill once more, never to regain his health. A prayer translated from his private diary captures his spirit of submission to God's will:

I thank thee from the bottom of my heart for this punishment, and but one thing now I request of thee – that thy holy and good Spirit may effect in me thy purpose . . . If I die, I will see and praise thee. If I recover, the rest of my life will flow a stream of gratitude, spent in thy service to the honour of thy name.

In 1845 Philipp returned to his home in Pesth. He longed to serve Christ even though confined to his bed. 'How happy would I be,' he exclaimed, 'if Christ intended to do anything through me, a poor weak man! O my God, make me a blessing on this bed of suffering and illness.' This prayer was abundantly answered. He had wished to be a teacher: surely he could teach children from his bed, he thought. So he began with one boy. Within a few days there were five, then seven, then ten. Not many weeks later thirty children were crammed into his bedroom. This was the only education many of these children, most of whom were Jewish, would receive. Philipp taught them openly from the Scriptures, drawing the attention of the parents to the fact that he was now a Christian. And still the numbers grew. Soon Philipp was obliged to rent a larger bedroom as over fifty young Jewish children crowded to his classes. When the Rabbi preached against his activities, the numbers dropped dramatically, but pressure from the children soon persuaded parents to allow them to return. Philipp loved these children, gaining their confidence and respect. Many became convinced of the truths of the New Testament Scriptures, and carried this light and understanding back to their Jewish homes.

But Philipp's condition was worsening. Possibly suffering from a skin cancer, he was subjected to tortuous pain as the surgeon probed the wounds on his legs. 'I wish I could bear the pain more patiently in those terrible moments', he wrote. 'God has driven me into deep straits, but, thanks be to him, he is educating me for heaven. His ways are dark. So long as we are down here in this valley, it is impossible to have a clear view of God's plans or ways; but from the summit of the mountain we shall be able to see it all.' Elizabeth, who was now nineteen, joined Philipp in his school, teaching the girls with skill and success. Soon the numbers rose to one hundred and twenty.

In 1848 the surgeon who had been treating Philipp's condition broke the news that the disease had now affected the bone and was incurable. God had long been preparing Philipp for this. Writing to Adolph, who was then studying in Edinburgh, he could rejoice in the prospect of eternity:

Dear Good Brother
Only a few words. God has laid me on a bed of sickness from which I will not rise again. So rejoice to know that I will be redeemed, freed from pain, saved – saved from care! I will be with Christ. What joy and delight! I am ready to depart; I rejoice in God. Pray for me. My whole body is ruined. In heaven there will be no pain. I praise the Lamb slain for us. So farewell.

During 1849 the calamitous Hungarian war raged though the country. Pesth was bombarded and many had to flee the city. Philipp was now weak and could not leave, but as he heard the tumult of warfare all around him, his spirit was calm. In one last letter written to Charles Schwartz, whose early ministry had profoundly influenced him, Philipp says:

I am happy. God has done great things for me. My body is decaying, but my inner man lives and grows. I am weak and miserable, scorched with the heat of affliction, but within I am strong in my God and rich in him who became poor for me. Heat takes away the dross and prepares a transcendent joy. I do not dread to die; the Conqueror of death has taken away its sting. I long after the house not made with hands, eternal in the heavens.

Philipp's sufferings increased until September when God at last granted him deliverance from that 'scorching heat of affliction' as he entered the 'transcendent joy'. His father and Elizabeth were with him the night he died. Noticing that Elizabeth was crying, Philipp called her, embraced her and said, 'Why do you weep? Look at me. I am a great deal better now. The Lord Jesus our Saviour is gracious and of great mercy.' And so he died, with his father kneeling by his side, praying. Writing to Adolph, Israel said: 'Our Philipp, my dearly beloved son and your faithful brother, is in heaven. We shall see him again.'

Elizabeth devoted herself to the work of Philipp's school. Since her conversion in 1843 she had applied herself with energy and perseverance to the task of influencing others to accept the same soul-transforming truths. Despite her self-effacing personality, she started prayer meetings at her school where her zeal earned her the nickname of 'Mad Elizabeth'. Her knowledge of the Scriptures was extensive and, like Adolph, she spent much time in secret prayer. Her part in Philipp's school was the crowning joy of Elizabeth's life and when he died she missed her brother sorely, but was determined that his school should continue.

Sadly, Elizabeth married a worthless man. He professed to be a Christian and appeared to have an interest in the school, but he mistreated and abused his gentle wife. Though Elizabeth made no complaint to her parents, her unhappy face and obvious depression troubled Israel and Henrietta. Questioned about her marriage, she would only reply that her husband did not quite understand her and she hoped he might improve.

But he did not improve. When Elizabeth's health began to break down, her parents brought her home to protect her from further harm and care for her. It was too late. Though Israel and his wife nursed Elizabeth day and night, she died in 1854 at the age of twenty-seven. Greatly loved by Jew and Gentile alike, Elizabeth's death caused widespread grief. Adolph too shared the sorrow. He had just completed his studies in Edinburgh and longed to return home, though he knew it was impossible for he would be immediately forced into military service.

But he wrote these words of his sister, Elizabeth:

My good sister Elizabeth died about a fortnight ago. We know she died in faith, love and hope. The grief and bereavement is on our side only. She was very noble and knew how to deny herself for the sake of God's kingdom. Next to Philipp I always admired her most. We are all going home – sooner or later; but may God grant us a long life if it so please him.

God heard Adolph's request and granted him many years of useful service for his kingdom. After his theological training at the Free Church College in Edinburgh, Adolph went to Belfast where he was ordained by the Irish Presbyterian Church as a missionary to the Jews. Here he married Sara Owen, who loved and watched over him with vigilant concern for the next thirty-seven years. Throughout his life the evangelisation of his own people was of paramount importance to Adolph, and his first missionary appointment was to the German city of Hamburg. But in God's purposes he was not destined to remain in missionary work, and this appointment terminated after an early disagreement with the Mission committee over the most effectual methods for influencing the Jews.

These circumstances led Saphir to return to Britain and in 1856 he began his first pastorate in South Shields. This was a formative period for the young preacher and here he wrote his first major book, entitled *Conversion*. His lucid experimental style makes this work and his subsequent titles still sought after among those who scour the second-hand bookshops and lists. Here, too, he was prepared for future usefulness by the discipline of suffering. The loss of an eighteen-month-old daughter, Asra, the only child of their marriage, was a grief Adolph could never recall without acute pain.

In 1861 Saphir began his London ministry; first at Greenwich until 1872, when a period of ill-health brought his pastorate to a close. This was perhaps the happiest and most productive period of Adolph's life. Late in 1872 he moved to West London where a new church building had recently become available in Notting Hill. Adolph's ministry quickly attracted a congregation of over a thousand worshippers. Spurgeon's astonishing ministry at the Metropolitan Tabernacle was also at its peak and brought the two men into frequent contact. Adolph held Spurgeon in the highest esteem, describing him as 'the genuine article . . . simple, straight, godly; and one who has not been led astray by any of the modern fads.' Both preached a warm, attractive and biblical Calvinism and both held the Scriptures as the unquestioned authority for all their preaching. A steady flow of books came from Saphir's active pen during this period, written from the vantage point of one thoroughly conversant with Jewish tradition and thought. *Christ in the Scriptures* and *Expository Lectures on the Epistle to the Hebrews* were among his best known.

Never strong, Adolph Saphir resigned from his London ministry in 1880 when he was only forty-nine years of age. Two or three short ministries followed, but in 1891 came a blow which his frail system could not sustain: the sudden death of his beloved Sara. For thirty-seven years they had been inseparable. Many now wondered how Adolph would manage without her, but it was a needless question. The day after her funeral he suffered a heart attack and died a few hours later on 5 April 1891. His last surviving sister and her husband were with him at the time; he was fifty-nine. His gravestone bears only a brief inscription but the accompanying text is one that Adolph himself would have chosen: 'I determined to know nothing among you, save Jesus Christ and him crucified.'

Spurgeon, whose own earthly course had only nine more months to run, spoke sadly of the loss of his friend in one of his final sermons: 'Our dearly beloved friend Adolph Saphir passed away last Saturday . . . the biblical student, the lover of the Word, the lover of the God of Israel.'

JANET
A Better Marriage Feast

Then he said to me, 'Write: "Blessed are those who are called to the marriage supper of the Lamb!"'

(Rev. 19:9)

Beyond the clamour of this sphere
A voice is calling calm and clear,
'Rise up, my child, and come away,
For winter days of pain are past,
Sweet flowers of spring appear at last;
Arise and come, the call obey;
From sorrow, strife and sin released,
Come, join the Lamb's glad marriage feast.'

F.C.

14

Any account of the triumphs of the grace of God in the lives of Christian men and women through times of adversity, must necessarily be drawn almost exclusively from the annals of church history. The inclusion of contemporary material is fraught with problems, not least lest it should lead to further suffering in the lives of those whom it concerns. But to exclude all such narratives on these grounds would leave an imbalanced and incomplete record. The details of Janet's short life and death are therefore included here, with the full co-operation of her parents, that we may be reminded that God still brings glory to his name by sustaining his people through their earthly trials, however severe these may be.

In May 1949 a healthy fair-haired baby girl was born in a London hospital: Eric and Sheila's first child; and Janet's birth brought all the joys and perplexities that first-born babies bring to their parents the world over. For two years there was nothing to indicate the difficulties this child would face in her life, but a serious and debilitating attack of measles, followed by bronchial pneumonia when Janet was two, left the cheerful toddler weak. When her strength at last began to return, Eric and Sheila responded to an invitation to stay with friends in Newquay, hoping this might rebuild the child's health. But within a day or two Janet fell ill once more. Pneumonia set in again, this time complicated by suspected asthma. Janet was now struggling for her life. The doctor who attended her later confessed that he feared she would never return to her own home.

Few drugs or alleviating inhalers were available in the early 1950s, but eventually the little girl regained a measure of strength and the family travelled back to London. Balcombe Street, adjacent to Baker Street, where they lived, was far from the ideal environment for an asthmatic child: steam from the trains as they hissed into Marylebone Station filled all the rooms in the flat and Janet's attacks of asthma gradually increased both in number and severity. The birth of a brother, Ian, when Janet was three, added to the problems that Eric and Sheila faced. For shortly after his birth Ian developed epileptic fits which left him mentally retarded.

So in 1953 the decision was taken to move from central London, and the family found property in Middlesex. Here the atmosphere was less polluted and Eric's job was still within fairly easy access. Though the outlook for the family seemed bleak, this move had been ordained in the providence of God for their greater good. Before long Eric and Sheila discovered that a near neighbour was a Christian. Her manner of life, concern and conversation startled and challenged them. Now they began to look beyond the sorrows and necessities of their present experience to the unseen and eternal. Through the influence of this neighbour both Eric and Sheila were converted. Young and inexperienced believers though they were, they now knew the source of spiritual strength to which they could resort in distress.

Janet was nearly of school age by this time, but her constant attacks of asthma put attendance at any normal school out of the question. At last, upon medical advice and at the suggestion of the local education department, it was decided that she must attend an open-air school and one on Hayling Island was designated. Choking back her tears, the child set off each term by coach for boarding school many miles distant. The discipline of suffering was already beginning to mould Janet's character.

By 1957, when Janet was nearly eight, Eric and Sheila felt that these grievous partings were too much for either Janet or themselves to bear any longer. Nor was Janet's health improving. They decided on another move: this time it would be to the south coast, and Eric would undertake the onerous task of commuting to central London each day.

Again the question of Janet's education posed a problem. Though clearly an intelligent child, she was too frail to attend a normal school. So an arrangement was made for a visiting teacher to call three times a week to give Janet home tuition. The discovery that this teacher was also a Christian gave added assurance of the constant care and mercies of their heavenly Father. Much of Janet's schoolwork was undertaken from her bed, yet she managed to maintain a standard of achievement comparable to that of other children of her age and ability.

Meanwhile Ian's condition and needs placed an ever-increasing burden on Sheila. Eric's long business hours meant that her only companion for much of the day was her invalid daughter. Ian, who was nearly six, was a strong little fellow in spite of his serious handicap. Janet did all she could to help her mother, though her brother's physical strength far outweighed her own. After ten months in their new home Ian's condition deteriorated rapidly. When he died, Janet's grief was deep and real. She had been devoted to him and his need had called out a degree of self-forgetfulness unusual in a child. She never forgot her little brother. Often when visiting his grave she would gather ox-eyed daisies and buttercups from a nearby field and place them there in his memory.

Janet was now nine and her own health remained a

source of constant anxiety. Shortly before Ian's death she had been admitted to hospital for the extraction of a tooth. Within two hours of the treatment she had become seriously ill; complications set in and one lung collapsed. To treat this condition, the child was obliged to remain in hospital for three weeks, lying with her head downwards. The lung, however, remained permanently damaged, and of little further use. Janet's asthma attacks now became more prolonged and debilitating. A severe one could last for three days or more; the struggle for breath leaving her weak and exhausted. During this period her condition involved at least seventeen spells in hospital, where she was often placed in an oxygen tent.

Janet bore it all with little complaint, but there were joys to compensate – joys trivial enough to some, but which brought Janet intense pleasure. A visit to the blue-bell woods was an event she never forgot. The sea of purple stretching out into the distance and the strong sweet scent of spring were delights she loved to recall. Her own little plot at the bottom of the garden brought immense enjoyment and when she was well enough she would walk down the garden to see how her plants were progressing. From her bedroom window she could watch the changing seasons, the birds that visited the garden, the waving corn in the field beyond, and on one occasion, she even had the thrill of watching a foal born.

When she was ten, Janet met someone who was destined in God's purposes to effect her life profoundly. Graham was a young theological student in training for the ministry, whose parents had recently retired to the south coast. His college vacations were spent with them and through a mutual friend he was introduced to Eric and Sheila. Alive to their spiritual needs, Graham offered to come to their home each week and teach them from the Scriptures whenever he was in the area. This he did, and of course soon met Janet. Each time Graham visited Eric and Sheila he would first go upstairs to Janet's bedroom to explain the Bible to her and pray with her.

By natural temperament, and through her sufferings, Janet had developed many commendable traits of character. But Graham set before her a perspective on her life and experiences that Janet had never before considered. From the first chapter of Genesis he pointed to the omnipotence and glory of the Creator under whose control rested the destiny of all created things. Janet's illness, therefore, was no mere accident: rather it was within God's special purpose for her. True faith was far more than a general acknowledgement of the being and goodness of God; it was a specific and personal response to the One revealed in Scripture. Whatever the outcome of her prolonged illness, whether it should mean further suffering or even death, she could then know that her heaven was sure.

More than this, Graham showed Janet that she too was a sinner by nature and by act, and apart from the saving grace of God, stood in imminent peril. Janet had never seen it like that before. Gradually she understood the implication of the things that Graham was telling her as the Spirit of God gave her insight and spiritual desires. One night Janet was clearly troubled, and, after Graham had finished talking with her, Sheila went upstairs to her daughter. She found her subdued and thoughtful: she spoke little, so Sheila prayed with her and settled her for the night. Later that evening, and before Graham left, Janet could be heard crying. She rarely cried and Sheila was naturally anxious to go to her. 'No,' said Graham wisely, 'leave her to cry. She is crying for her sins', and then he added significantly, 'I feel she is very near the kingdom.'

Early the following morning, long before Janet would

normally be awake, Sheila again heard her crying. This time she slipped into her room, but found the tears were tears of joy. 'O Mummy!' she exclaimed, 'Jesus died for me!' Words seemed strangely inadequate to Sheila as she wiped the child's tears and knelt beside her bed, holding her hand.

The change in Janet was real and obvious. Now she would spend hours reading her Bible – she read it through from the beginning – marking passages which she felt were of special significance to herself. Great was her delight when Graham arrived one night with a bulky parcel for her. Unwrapping it, she discovered a large and handsome volume entitled *The Child's Story Bible*. Written by Catherine Vos, this collection (now published as three separate books) retold the familiar stories vividly, using the narrative to stress important biblical truths. Attractively interspersed with illustrations, the volume brought Janet hours of pleasure.

But there were problems too. Like many other Christians, Janet was disturbed by a nagging doubt lest her profession of faith should not be genuine after all. Confiding her fear to Graham, she listened carefully as he demonstrated from the First Epistle of John the different 'tests' she might apply to herself to dispel her fears, particularly drawing her attention to the use of the word 'know' in the epistle. These verses she underlined carefully.

Janet's condition was now more stable, due partly to the benefits derived from more advanced medication. For the first time, it was decided, she should attend a normal school when she was well enough. Overjoyed, Janet entered enthusiastically into school activities and quickly became popular among the other girls, who vied with each other to protect her. Inevitably there were periods when Janet could not attend, but she was seldom at a loss for things to do. Puzzles, poems, competitions: she was always busy, and would compile little notebooks, many containing her secret thoughts on passages of Scripture she had read. One cherished ambition was to write a life of the Apostle Paul. A life of suffering, courageously borne for the sake of Christ and the gospel he preached, appealed to Janet: her own sufferings gave her a certain empathy with the man who could say, 'When I am weak, then am I strong.' Together she and her mother discussed the forthcoming work, making careful notes of his journeys and experiences. When Janet began to write, she chose as her theme the Apostle's words: 'Lest I should be exalted above measure . . . there was given me a thorn in the flesh, the messenger of Satan to buffet me.'

One day a special letter came with the morning post: a wedding invitation. Graham was to marry and Janet and her parents were invited to the wedding. She had already met Graham's bride and approved of his choice. This would be the first wedding she had attended and Janet was highly excited. What should she wear? She began to think and plan for the important day, 15 April 1961. Sheila set off and bought herself a new pink hat, a hat which Janet thought made her mother look lovely. Spring had come early that year, clothing the hedgerows and trees in tender green; daffodils flowered jauntily in the gardens: the world seemed alive with hopefulness and joy.

But two weeks before the wedding Janet had a severe attack of asthma. It left her weakened and subdued and she began to fear that she might not be well enough to undertake the journey, with all the lengthy celebrations to follow. Sensitive by nature, Janet could see that her parents were anxious about her condition. Turning to her mother, she asked, 'Mummy, why are you worrying? You must trust; I am not worrying.' And still she prayed each night that she might be well enough to attend the wedding. At last April 14 dawned; final plans were made and everything was ready. Janet went cheerfully to bed in high anticipation. But during the night Sheila heard a sound she had learnt to dread: Janet struggling for breath.

Instinctively Sheila knew it would be a bad attack and though Janet never called out in the night, neither she nor Eric would leave her alone at these times. And so the long vigil began. When morning broke – the morning of the wedding – the doctor was summoned. How many times he came and went that day they never knew, for Janet was very ill. 'O Mummy,' she gasped, when she managed to gain a moment's respite, 'I am so very sorry, I have made you miss Graham's wedding, and you did buy that lovely pink hat.' Characteristically her concern and thought was for others, even in such a moment of crisis. Writing long afterwards, her mother was to say, 'All her bravery and deep love for her Saviour, I find impossible to express.'

The attack became one of the worst Sheila had ever seen. All day she and Eric held the child, trying to support her as she fought for breath. It had been hours since Janet had last spoken; then quite suddenly at three in the afternoon she sat bolt upright, her expression changed, and on her face came a look of painful joy. Fixing her eyes steadily in one direction, she called out in a loud voice, 'It's all right, Ian, I'm coming.' Sinking back into her mother's arms, she resumed her long battle for breath.

By eight o'clock in the evening the ferocity of the attack seemed to be passing. No-one had eaten all day, and as Janet's breathing had eased, Eric went downstairs to prepare a meal. Quite suddenly Janet turned, flung her arms around her mother and exclaimed, 'O Mummy, I love you *so* much!' Then it seemed she was not breathing at all. Eric responded quickly to Sheila's cry for help, the doctor was hastily recalled: but Janet had gone – called to a better marriage feast – the marriage supper of the Lamb.

Bibliography
& Suggested Further Reading

Bibliography
(and Suggested Further Reading)

1. JOHN BRADFORD

Foxe, John. *Book of Martyrs, The Acts and Monuments of the Church*. London, 1875.

Loane, Marcus. *Pioneers of the Reformation in England*. The Church Bookroom Press, 1964.

Ryle, J. C. *Five English Reformers*. London: The Banner of Truth Trust, 1965.

2. RICHARD AND ALLAN CAMERON

Blaikie, W. G. *The Preachers of Scotland*. Cunningham Lectures, 1888.

Herkless, John. *Richard Cameron*. Famous Scot Series, 1896.

3. WANG MING-DAO

Brother David with Sara Bruce and Lela Gilbert. *Walking the Hard Road*. Marshall Pickering, 1989.

Lambert, Tony. *The Resurrection of the Chinese Church*. Hodder and Stoughton and Overseas Missionary Fellowship, 1991.

Lyall, Leslie. *Come Wind, Come Weather*. Hodder and Stoughton, 1961.

Ming-Dao, Wang. *A Stone Made Smooth*. Southampton: Mayflower Christian Books, 1981.

4. SUSANNAH SPURGEON

Autobiography of C. H. Spurgeon. Vol. 1, *The Early Years* and vol. 2, *The Full Harvest*. Edinburgh: The Banner of Truth Trust, 1962 and 1973.

Ray, Charles. *Mrs CHS*. Passmore and Alabaster, 1903.
Spurgeon, Susannah. *Ten Years of my Life and Ten Years After*.
  Passmore and Alabaster, 1885 and 1895.

5. THOMAS HOG

Memoirs of Veitch, Hog, etc. Edinburgh, 1846.

6. MONICA

The Confessions of S. Augustine. Library of the Fathers, translated by E. B. Pusey, Oxford, 1840.
Farrer, F. W. *Lives of the Fathers*. Edinburgh: A. and C. Black,
  vol. 1, 1889.

7. MARGARET BAXTER

The Autobiography of Richard Baxter. J. M. Dent, 1974. Repr.
  London: Everyman's Library, 1985.
Wilkinson, J. T. *Richard Baxter and Margaret Charlton* (with,
  Richard Baxter, *The Breviate of the Life of Margaret Baxter*).
  London: Allen & Unwin, 1928.

8. JOHN OXTOBY

Leigh, Harvey. *'Praying Johnny'; or the Life and Labours of
  John Oxtoby, Primitive Methodist Preacher*. London, 1856.
Ritson, Joseph. *The Romance of Primitive Methodism*. London,
  1909.

9. EDWARD PAYSON

The Complete Works of Edward Payson, D.D. Compiled and
  edited by Asa Cummings, Portland, USA, 1846. Repr.
  Sprinkle Publications, 1984.
Memoir of the late Rev. Edward Payson. (anon.) Edinburgh,
  1852.
Prentiss, G. L. *The Life and Letters of Elizabeth Prentiss*.
  Hodder and Stoughton, 1881.

10. CATHERINE BOSTON

Memoirs of Thomas Boston. Edinburgh: The Banner of Truth Trust, 1988.

Watson, Jean. *The Pastor of Ettrick: Thomas Boston.* Edinburgh, 1883.

11. WILLIAM BRAMWELL

Sigston, James. *Memoir of Mr. W. Bramwell.* New York, 1820.

Stevens, Abel. *The History of Methodism.* London, 1861.

12. ALLEN GARDINER

Marsh, John W. *The Story of Commander Allen Gardiner, R.N.* 1888.

Page, Jessie. *Captain Allen Gardiner: Sailor and Saint.* London: Partridge & Co.

Thompson, Phyllis. *An Unquenchable Flame.* Hodder and Stoughton, 1983.

13. THE SAPHIR FAMILY

Carlyle, Gavin. *Mighty in the Scriptures – A Memoir of Adolph Saphir, D.D.* London: Shaw, 1893.